PENGUIN BOOKS

Kraftwerk

Uwe Schütte is a Reader in German at Aston University, Birmingham, where he teaches and researches contemporary Austrian and German literature, the writer W. G. Sebald and German popular music.

UWE SCHÜTTE

Kraftwerk

Future Music from Germany

PENGUIN BOOKS

PENGUIN BOOKS

UK | USA | Canada | Ireland | Australia
India | New Zealand | South Africa

Penguin Books is part of the Penguin Random House group of companies
whose addresses can be found at global.penguinrandomhouse.com

First published 2020
010

Set in 11.2/15.2 pt Haarlemmer MT Pro
Typeset by Jouve (UK), Milton Keynes
Printed and bound in Great Britain by Clays Ltd, Elcograf S.p.A.

A CIP catalogue record for this book is available from the British Library

ISBN: 978–0–141–98675–3

www.greenpenguin.co.uk

Penguin Random House is committed to a
sustainable future for our business, our readers
and our planet. This book is made from Forest
Stewardship Council® certified paper.

CONTENTS

Foreword vii

1. Introduction: The Birth of Electronic Pop Music in Düsseldorf 1

2. Early Works: The Kraftwerk Story Unfolds 29

3. Movement and Velocity: From *Autobahn* to *Trans-Europe Express* 49

4. 'We are the Robots': From *The Man-Machine* to *Computer World* 111

5. Enter the Digital Revolution: From *Techno Pop* to *Tour de France* 165

6. Sound and Vision 3D: Working on *The Catalogue* 207

7. 'Music Non Stop': Kraftwerk's Legacy 251

8. Postscript: 1 2 3 4 5 6 7 8 281

Acknowledgements 287
Notes 291

STALLS STANDING
03634
KRAFTWERK
SATURDAY 20 MARCH 2004
BRIXTON ACADEMY
TICKETS £22.50adv
DOORS: 6:30pm > KRAFTWERK ON STAGE 8:00pm
CURFEW 10:00pm
NO SUPPORT
A STRAIGHT PRESENTATION IN ASSOCIATION WITH HELTER SKELTER

FOREWORD

This general introduction to the astounding phenomenon that is Kraftwerk is the result of four pivotal moments in my life. It all began the first time I heard 'Autobahn' on the radio. I was probably eight or nine years old at the time, and the song could not fail to make an impression on me, a German boy always dreading my parents taking me for a drive on the motorway – I suffered from severe car sickness, and of course you are not allowed to stop when driving on the *Autobahn*.

The unusual German band name also stuck. Meaning 'power station' in English, Kraftwerk was an unusual choice of name for a pop band, Also, the lyrics were in German. Pop music inevitably meant English lyrics, which I could not understand, save for the few obvious key words. Pop bands always came from Britain or the US: Elvis, The Beatles, Buddy Holly and a few others were the musical heroes of my childhood and early-teen years. Though the small provincial town in which I grew up was only just over a hundred kilometres from Düsseldorf, where Kraftwerk were working in their Kling Klang studio, my next brush with their music came about four years later.

By then, we had moved into a village in rural Bavaria. Unhappy and an outsider among the village youth, I holed up in my room, busying myself with collecting stamps, reading and listening to music. My first record player was a gift from a kind neighbour who passed it on when she got a new one. I must have been about twelve years old then. Now I needed records of my own to play on my pretty, though modest, portable player.

I bought a copy of Deep Purple's *In Rock* and Kraftwerk's *Radio-Aktivität* (*Radio-Activity*) from a schoolfriend. I loved both. The latter featured some pretty odd cover artwork: it looked like an outdated Nazi radio set. Because it was an outdated Nazi radio set . How weird! Pop music on an album whose artwork imitated one of Hitler's instruments of propaganda. But then, Kraftwerk's music was neither pop nor rock – that much I understood. The album sounded more like a radio play, an odd transmission from a future past, containing some pop tunes and lots of strange noises and sounds. It was odd, too, in that it praised nuclear energy, which many people in Germany strongly opposed at the time.

I listened to *Radio-Aktivität* for many years and never grew tired of it. When and where my vinyl copy disappeared out of my life I can't recall. I probably sold it at the point when CDs became all the rage. For several years, I didn't bother with Kraftwerk, and this was the period in which they released one groundbreaking album after another. Needless to say, I deeply regret my stupidity in flogging my copy of *Radio-Aktivität*. Whenever I come across the album now in a second-hand-record shop, I check the inner sleeve to see if it has my name on it, in my immature handwriting from some forty years ago.

My next meaningful encounter with Kraftwerk happened about a decade later. I was a university student in the late eighties and at some point I saw a scruffy poster in a Munich second-hand-record shop. It looked strangely familiar, like a cheap reprint of a coloured photograph from sometime around the thirties, and showed four men wearing neat suits and sitting at a table underneath a tree. A very German image. Despite its nostalgic look, I recognized the group of men – they were the members of Kraftwerk.

The peculiar juxtaposition of a retro photograph and futurist, avant-garde electronic music immediately made an impression on me. At the time, I had been listening to all sorts of music – neoclassical New Music, jazz on the avant-gardist ECM label, US punk and English indie rock – but not

Kraftwerk. Seeing this image on the poster rekindled my interest, and I had also read several times about Kraftwerk's considerable influence on the British and American electronic music I was listening to at the time.

What's more, I felt that the incongruous poster expressed something deeply complex about my country and the difficulties I and my friends had with being German: a strange feeling of not being part of the country's history and its national identity, which was overshadowed so harrowingly by the crimes of the Holocaust and the horrors of the Second World War. Yet there was also a comforting sense of belonging to a naïve, childhood version of the country – an innocent, prosperous, positive Germany, as it were. A socially just Germany that allowed my refugee mum and working-class dad to work their way up the social ladder to enjoy the materialistic comforts of the middle class and enabled me to have a good education. The enervation triggered by the poster led me to hunt for more Kraftwerk in the shop. And I was lucky, digging out a cassette of their then most recent album, *Electric Cafe*, from 1986.

Fast-forward two decades. The final turning point in my relationship with Kraftwerk came in London on 20 March 2004 – the night they played the Brixton Academy. By then, I was a university lecturer. As I had never seen Kraftwerk live before, or even listened to a bootleg tape of one of their concerts, I was very much looking forward to finally being able to see them. Ticket sales started online just when I was scheduled to teach a class on German history to first-year undergraduate students. Needless to say, I was a little late. Fortunately, it took me only five minutes to get hold of two tickets.

On the evening of the concert, my partner didn't feel too well, but she decided to come along anyway. I vividly remember my heart pounding in anticipation. At precisely 8 p.m. the lights went out and a robotic voice announced the band in German; I hadn't been so excited about seeing a concert since my teenage years and had forgotten how physically energized you could get about going to a live performance.

Even though I had no clue what to expect, the show lived up to my expectations, which were considerable – the songs were immediately recognizable but sounded very contemporary and up to date; the visuals were fascinating to watch, interacting with the music in various ways; finally, the pristine electronic sound just blew me away. I had never heard anything like it before. Oh, and I should also mention that my girlfriend – now my wife – experienced a miraculous recovery during the concert. Maybe it was the power of the music.

Ever since that gig in Brixton, Kraftwerk have been on my mind and on my CD player. But I pursued my interest in the band only occasionally, for instance by reading the books in both German and English that had been written about them. I published a few journalistic pieces, mostly reviews of new releases such as the live album *Minimum-Maximum* (2005) and the *Catalogue* (2009) box set. More recently, I also decided to do some academic work on Kraftwerk.

In late 2014 I organized an afternoon discussion group, hoping to find maybe three or four British colleagues who might be interested in presenting a paper on Kraftwerk. I didn't anticipate the overwhelming response. In the end, a two-day conference was held in January 2015 at the university where I teach. It was sold out, the audience consisting of about two hundred Kraftwerk enthusiasts, some of whom had travelled from as far away as Denmark, Spain, Belgium, Germany and the United States. There was immense media interest in the conference, with several national papers and various radio channels asking for interviews or reporting from it. BBC Breakfast TV sent a camera team, and broadcast their report to several million viewers.

A second conference, which took place in Düsseldorf, the home of Kraftwerk, followed in October of that year, and the result of both conferences was a book in German that gave a comprehensive overview of Kraftwerk's discography and contained the best papers. However, given the considerable interest in Kraftwerk in the Anglophone world, I felt that an English-language introduction to the band was called for. This is it.

What to Expect

My approach in this book is to look at Kraftwerk not just as a band but rather as a cultural phenomenon, as an art project and concept translated into a multimedia combination of sound and image, graphic design and performance. The driving force behind what turned out to be Germany's most important cultural contribution to the field of popular music was the duo Ralf Hütter and Florian Schneider, who founded Kraftwerk in 1970.

Hütter, born in 1946, and Schneider, in 1947, belonged to the first post-war generation, a generation that broke with the nationalist and chauvinistic tradition that had dominated Germany for the previous two hundred years. Along with their peers, Hütter and Schneider sought to define a new German identity; their artistic and musical work with Kraftwerk was intended as a contribution to the political, cultural and moral rebuilding of Germany in the aftermath of Nazi atrocities.

Unlike existing books on Kraftwerk, I am not simply providing a history of the band; I'll also discuss aspects of their work such as graphic design and the band's visual presentation. In addition, I'll explore their art-historical background and the artistic context without which it is impossible to fully understand Kraftwerk. My focus is firmly on the audiovisual art package that is Kraftwerk, so this book will take only a very limited interest in gossip regarding personal quarrels, biographical issues and tales of human shortcomings.

Karl Bartos and Wolfgang Flür, members of Kraftwerk during their 'classic' phase from 1974 to the mid-eighties, made valuable contributions to the Kraftwerk project which were then sidelined by Hütter and Schneider. Both have written memoirs to put their side of the story to the public. I have used reliable information from Bartos's autobiography for this book; readers more interested in gossip and anecdotes should consult Flür's revelations.[1]

I have aimed to make this introduction to Kraftwerk accessible. Quotations from other literature on Kraftwerk have been kept to a minimum to make the book as readable as possible. As well as the English-language interviews cited in the existing books, I've made ample use of various articles on Kraftwerk, interviews with the band, and other pertinent sources in German. I trust that this, too, will shed – at least in part – a new light on the band for an Anglophone readership. Working on this book was a pleasure, and, in a way, it has constituted the fifth time my life has been irrevocably touched by the phenomenon of Kraftwerk.

I. INTRODUCTION:
THE BIRTH OF ELECTRONIC
POP MUSIC IN DÜSSELDORF

View of Düsseldorf city centre in 1945, showing the
bombing-raid damage.

'We compose the melodies by humming in our studio, and the rhythm comes from the noises of the machines.'

– Ralf Hütter

'Where is the 21st-century equivalent of Kraftwerk?'[1] asks the perplexed cultural critic Mark Fisher – and rightly so. Perhaps it is unfair to expect a pop band to be able to point us towards the future of music. Kraftwerk, however, managed this visionary feat. 'This was music with no guitars at all, no indebtedness to the blues, no appeal to any of the basic motivations behind so much pop music such as who to love, and, essentially, no frontman for the audience to identify with,' writes Kraftwerk biographer David Buckley. Kraftwerk was 'a complete theoretical annihilation of most of the precedents and tenets on which modern rock music was based'.[2]

The optimistic, futuristic music they began producing more than four decades ago in their dingy studio in the red-light district of Düsseldorf has turned out to be the soundtrack of our twenty-first-century present. Just open your ears: the idea of using machines to make electronic music has been deeply imprinted on the DNA of contemporary pop music since the eighties. British synth-pop, dance-music styles like techno and house, experimental electronica and Japanese bubblegum pop have all, in one way or another, been influenced by Kraftwerk. The band's importance has not waned – the work of current artists as diverse as Daft Punk, Jay-Z and Coldplay, musical heroes such as David Bowie, as well as underground acts like Laibach,[3] all attest to the lasting relevance of Kraftwerk.

Mark Fisher's question could thus be answered by pointing out that there is no need for an equivalent of Kraftwerk in today's musical landscape, because Kraftwerk's sound is ubiquitous. But then, that isn't what his question was aiming at. What he wanted to know is: Why aren't there any bands or artists around that make music which completely breaks with the rules, conventions and patterns that govern pop music as we know it? Music which, by sounding utterly different, would constitute proof that there exists a potential for the arrival of something genuinely new – socially, politically or culturally. Instead, what is sold to us is just the repetition, variation and regurgitation of the existing: a repackaged version of the past.

The explanation is simple: there exists no music of the future today, because there is no longer any such thing as a future. The future, according to

Fisher, has been cancelled. The historical struggle for a better world has always been driven by the promise of better things to come. When The Beatles promised such a prospect in their 1967 song 'Getting Better', they really meant it. The song caught the optimistic mood of the rebellious generation of the late sixties. By the end of the twentieth century these high hopes had waned. Today, when thinking about tomorrow, we see more threat than opportunity, given the current climate of economic crisis, global warming, political demagogy and the erosion of democratic values. How could we possibly imagine building a better future?

The state of the 'futuristic' in art demonstrates this. Hasn't it turned into an established style that has ceased to refer to any future we expect to be markedly different from our present? Equally, the predominantly bright future promised by Kraftwerk's more optimistic music of the seventies has failed to materialize in the twenty-first century. Yes, we live in a 'computer world', as the title of their 1981 album anticipated, but as they also predicted, government agencies misuse digitalization to invade our privacy and corrode our civil rights. And today there is no 'Europe Endless', as celebrated on the opening track of the 1977 album, *Trans-Europe Express*, but instead the bleak reality of Brexit and the foolish determination of Europhobic sections of society to sever political and economic ties with Europe.

'We are from Deutschland'

Perceptions of Germans and German culture in the UK continue to be dogged by old stereotypes. It is hardly a coincidence that Rammstein are the most commercially successful German musical act in Britain. Their scheme to peddle silly Teutonic clichés about Germany and satisfy the prejudices of their fans pays off neatly. Tellingly, Rammstein are very popular not *despite* the fact that the vast majority of their audience don't understand the language they are singing in, but because of it. It is enough that they turn it into the parodic representation of the Nazi Germans seen in war films.

Now consider Kraftwerk: arguably the most critically acclaimed and influential German band in the Anglophone world, they also achieved popularity by playing upon their German identity – though in a dissimilar way to Rammstein. What Kraftwerk were aiming to achieve was not to exploit their Germanness but to forge a new German identity, often by ironically subverting clichés while simultaneously being serious about their heritage. That Kraftwerk seemed prototypically German when they emerged on the scene was confirmed by the German media and fellow German musicians. Michael Karoli, the guitarist from Can, said: 'Kraftwerk were very German. I think we were more open.'[4] What he refers to here, and rightly so, is Can's eagerness to assimilate musical inspirations from across the world, as evidenced in their unique fusion of experimental music, jazz, New Music, African rhythms and improvisation.

Kraftwerk, in contrast, eschewed such cosmopolitan musical influences, as well as the Anglo-American tradition of music (even though, privately, they were avid fans of acts such as The Beach Boys, James Brown, Iggy and The Stooges, and The Doors). 'We have a Teutonic rhythm, really Germanic,'[5] Ralf Hütter claimed. But what is that supposed to mean, a 'Teutonic rhythm'? It is basically no more than flirting with stereotypes, a calculated statement aiming to create a unique selling point for Kraftwerk. Hütter and Schneider openly admitted this: 'We came from a country which evokes a certain type of imagery, a lot of clichés, so let's play this game, let's transform ourselves into these stereotypes.'[6]

Today, this tried-and-tested pop-music stratagem is called 'subversive over-identification' – just think of Laibach or (the better part of) gangsta rap.

The matter is a complex one, and difficult to disentangle. In interviews, particularly at the beginning of their career, the members of Kraftwerk purposefully allude to their emphatic Germanness, thereby in turn inviting descriptions that reinforced the perception of them as stereotypically German. This mechanism exists in both the German and the English media. For example, the German journalist Christoph Dallach once said to Hütter: 'Kraftwerk, with due respect, is reckoned to be a typically German band abroad: distanced, cold, perfectionist and highly effective.'[7]

Much of the German press still continues to describe the band in such terms, the staple characteristics being 'cool' and 'cold',[8] 'minimal emotional, callous and bureaucratic'.[9] Military imagery in the vein of 'the human as missile, as a Teutonic machine [. . .], detached and motorized'[10] is sometimes utilized. British and American journalists follow suit, of course, and identify all sorts of traits deemed to be typically German: 'Kraftwerk's sound is precise, efficient, emotionally cold and technologically advanced,'[11] wrote Alexis Petridis. Meanwhile, Mark Richardson in his review of the 2005 live album, *Minimum-Maximum*, pointed out that their work is characterized by a 'precise, economical aesthetic'.[12]

Kraftwerk have always stressed that they are

from Germany – but not because they were proud of this, or at all nationalist. Far from it. It is important to understand that their use of Germanness stems from a very German problem – the problem of national identity after the Nazi era. Speaking in 1976, Hütter said: 'There's a whole generation in Germany, between [the ages of] 30 and 50, that has lost its own identity, and that never even had any.'[13] He also explained: 'There was really no German culture after the war. Everyone was rebuilding their homes and getting their little Volkswagens. In the clubs when we first started playing, you never heard a German record, you switched on the radio and all you heard was Anglo-American music, you went to the cinema and all the films were Italian and French. That's okay, but we needed our own cultural identity.'[14]

In 1974, Ralf Hütter and Florian Schneider took the plunge and decided to feature German lyrics on their game-changing track 'Autobahn'. This decision amounted to a political gesture: Kraftwerk made 'a virtue out of their nationality rather than concealing it under an Anglo-American veneer'[15] like the vast majority of their German contemporaries, who either opted for an English band name (for example, Tangerine Dream) or featured non-German singers (for example, Can) or simply aped Anglo-American pop music by singing in English (for example, Faust, Ash Ra Tempel and Birth Control). By using their own language and actively celebrating their national identity, Kraftwerk were 'articulating the mood of Germany's post-war generation – it was time to reclaim German culture from the dark shadows of recent history and move forward'.[16] Forward into a future that, given the dark horrors of the recent past, must inevitably be brighter.

The phenomenon of an internationally revered German band or writer (or other artist) failing to receive equivalent recognition in their native country is not as rare as Anglophone observers might expect. 'The Germans never do appreciate what's on their own doorstep,' Mark E. Smith, late lead singer of The Fall, remarked in conversation with Irmin Schmidt, keyboard player of Can.[17] He is right: this perplexing attitude is rooted in an inferiority complex that haunts German culture in realms that stretch beyond home-grown pop music.[18]

What might also not be obvious from a British perspective is that – at least as far as the educated classes are concerned – being German automatically means feeling European. German and European identity don't clash but instead complement each other. After its defeat in the Second World War, Germany's identification with the idea of Europe provided a way out of the moral and political disrepute into which it had fallen. The country was eager to show that it no longer aspired to supremacy but instead to cooperation – peace rather than war and territorial expansion. Kraftwerk are a case in point for this German trait; their 1977 album, *Trans-Europe Express*, which celebrates trans-European train travel and cultural exchange, is the clearest indicator of the inherent European identity that defines the work of the band and the attitudes of the polylingual Hütter and Schneider.

In fact, the transition from *Autobahn* (1974) to their last studio album, *Tour de France* (2003), along with the successive reduction of the German language in their work, replaced by various foreign languages from French to Spanish to Russian, echoes the wider political development of European integration after the Second World War. It also reflects the importance of cultural influences outside the German tradition: Russian supremacism, US pop art, Italian Futurism, French cycling culture, and so on.

This merging of different traditions finds a parallel in the synthesis of various art forms that comprises the Kraftwerk œuvre. As Ralf Hütter pointed out in 2006: 'The ideas reflected in our work are both internationalism and the mixing of different art forms. It's the idea that you don't separate dance over here and architecture over there, painting over there. We do everything, and the marriage of art and technology was Kraftwerk right from the beginning.'[19]

Düsseldorf

Identification with the political vision of a peaceful Europe was one way of dealing with the problem of being German in the aftermath of fascism. Identification with local traditions provided another route. Both Hütter and Schneider have strong allegiances to their roots, and to this day they have not moved from the locality where they were born. Traditionally, the Rhineland was a heavily industrialized region, due to its natural coal resources and steel industry. The area has always been staunchly Catholic, with the impressive cathedral in Cologne acting as the spiritual centre of the faith.

Another strong tradition is the collective madness of the *rheinischer Karneval*, a festivity of alcohol-fuelled shenanigans that climaxes annually in February or March and creates a sort of exceptional state of emergency in the two most important cities of the Rhineland: Cologne and Düsseldorf. Both engage in a (more or less friendly) rivalry that may be compared to that between Manchester and Liverpool, or Glasgow and Edinburgh – and this rivalry extends to clashes between fans of Kraftwerk and Can over which is the better band.

While Cologne is often considered by Germans to have the edge over Düsseldorf culturally, the latter has of late been recognized as the home of German electronic pop music, due in part to Kraftwerk, but certainly not entirely. In *Electri_City: The Düsseldorf School of Electronic Music* (2014), a book of oral history, Rudi Esch, formerly bass player of Düsseldorf industrial outfit Die Krupps, made a convincing case that the city is indeed Germany's 'capital of electronic music' (and therefore, one might add, Europe's, too). Alongside Kraftwerk – and their off-shoots Neu! and La Düsseldorf – DAF, Der Plan, Propaganda and Rheingold have also put the city on the musical map.

After the Second World War Allied bombing campaigns left Cologne and Düsseldorf largely destroyed. Germany was carved up into four zones among the victorious Allies and the Rhineland region fell under British military occupation. When West Germany was founded in 1949 as a result of the Cold War rift between the three Western Allies and the Soviet Union, it was decided that the new (provisional) capital of the Federal Republic would be located in the small town of Bonn on the river Rhine, some 30 kilometres south of Cologne. The first chancellor of Germany, the conservative and staunchly Catholic Konrad Adenauer, had been mayor of Cologne until he was removed by the Nazis when they came to power in 1933.

Hütter and Schneider hence grew up in a region that had become the new centre of political power in Germany. With the *Wirtschaftswunder* (economic miracle) soon under way, the Rhineland flourished economically, too, with thriving businesses and prospering industry turning it into a wealthy region. The comfortable circumstances in which they both grew up was due to their parents benefiting from these economic developments. As we'll see, their wealthy background played no small role when it came to the decision to spend money on very expensive early electronic-music gear.

In order to counter the centralized structures that had existed under both the Kaiser and the Nazi dictatorship, a federal model was implemented in Germany. Adapting the US system, eleven *Bundesländer* (federal states) were founded by the Allies. Nordrhein-Westfalen (North Rhine Westphalia), or NRW for short, was one of the largest, and is still the most populous federal state. Its infrastructure was quickly modernized, including the creation of a dense network of *Autobahns* to connect the cities in the conurbation area (Düsseldorf, Dortmund, Essen, Bochum, Duisburg). In fact, the first *Reichsautobahn*, linking Cologne and Bonn, had already been built between 1929 and 1932 (that is, before the Nazis rose to power in 1933).

Düsseldorf was chosen as the state capital of this highly modernized industrial region. The city itself, however, became known for sectors far more glamorous than manufacturing, including fashion, advertising and media, the influential Academy of Art and a network of galleries, the financial sector and the upmarket shopping boulevard Königsallee in the city centre. In his cod screenplay *Am Diskö mit Kraftwerk* from 1978, the British author and film maker Chris Petit makes a fictional Kraftwerk declare: 'We are completely isolated because Düsseldorf is a city of offices, the bureaucratic centre of German industry.'[20]

Well, it wasn't quite like that for Hütter and Schneider, but it is very true that Düsseldorf was and remains a city of offices, agencies and shops rather than one of factories and collieries, as could be found all over the Rhineland. In one of his many statements intended to be taken with a pinch of salt,

Hütter once claimed: 'We work a lot. We improvise and create new pieces. The very clean atmosphere of the city still stimulates us.'[21]

Düsseldorf also served as an administrative base for the British Army of the Rhine (BAOR), which was stationed in the region between 1945 and 1994, first as an occupying force, then as part of NATO's efforts to deter the Soviet Union from invading Germany during the Cold War. Inevitably, the long-term presence of British troops left its traces on the culture of the city, as the army brought along its own infrastructure for the soldiers. Local businesses in Düsseldorf would cater for the troops, their families and visitors from Britain; for example, bars would sell English beer. Crucially, the army had its own radio station: the British Forces Broadcasting Service (BFBS), featuring British DJs playing music that was perhaps not available in record shops or heard on German radio programmes.

For a young German generation opposed to the conservative values of the Adenauer governments and to the blind eye of the ruling elite in regard to former Nazis (who simply continued their careers in leading positions in society), English-language pop music became a vehicle of protest and rebellion against the authorities, which still clung to hostile views regarding 'foreign' culture. Listening to Elvis was enough to provoke parents, teachers and neighbours who still favoured conservative (some might say reactionary) *Schlager* music, the easy-listening tunes popular at the time.

To immerse oneself in Anglo-American pop music seemed a suitable and enjoyable means of expressing opposition to a system in which Nazi thinking could continue unchallenged in the police force, the judicial system and educational institutions. The eminent German pop-music scholar Diedrich Diedrichsen once described the act of listening to Anglo-American music at this time as a form of cultural de-Nazification.

Hütter and Schneider, however, belonged to the smaller group of people who were unhappy that the young post-war German generation possessed no culture of its own, only pale imitations of Anglo-American models. A new, genuinely autonomous type of music was needed to express a new German identity, one that rejected the values propagated by Nazism and by Christian conservatism. Inevitably, it had to be constructed from scratch, though it could look back to the great modernist tradition that existed in Germany before it was cut short by fascism. And so Krautrock was born.

Kraftwerk, in particular, saw the need to anchor their vision of an authentic German music in their regional surroundings and traditions – 'ethnic music from the Rhine-Ruhr area',[22] as Florian Schneider put it. Ralf Hütter stated more precisely: 'Country music, for example, is an impression of life which belongs to Texas. This music, however, has nothing to do with Düsseldorf. We have always understood our music as specifically industrial music. And, therefore, also as ethnic music.'[23] Sounds from home – or 'Heimatklänge', to quote the title of a track on their third album, *Ralf and Florian* (1973).

The notion of 'ethnic music' should under no circumstances be understood as crypto-nationalist. Rather, it is crucial to understand that Kraftwerk's music reflected a multilayered identity. On one level, it stood for a strong regional identity: sophisticated Düsseldorf and the industrialized Rhine-Ruhr region as their immediate *Heimat*;[24] on another level, it represented their ambivalent national identity as Germans (which comprised the rejected historical legacy of fascism); and finally, it embodied their European and, in an extended sense, internationalist identity as what would now be called 'global citizens'.

The Thriving Düsseldorf Art Scene

The Düsseldorf art scene at the time was ripe with new artistic ideas, high concepts and revolutionary initiatives, an exciting melting-pot in which new approaches to art cross-pollinated. Working alongside local luminaries such as Joseph Beuys and Jörg Immendorff influenced Hütter and Schneider's decision to make music inspired by conceptual art. Performing among and for artists as well as art aficionados put them in close touch with what was happening in the thriving art scene of the late sixties and early seventies.

The hub of this scene was the Creamcheese club, located close to the Academy of Arts. Hütter and Schneider were regulars and local artists were responsible for the unusual interior design of the establishment – for instance, its 20-metre-long bar and twenty-four TV sets, on continuously and showing different channels. The Creamcheese was home to various artworks, such as Günther Uecker's installation *Electric Garden* (an outsized nail housed in a metal cage alongside several neon lights) and hosted concerts by British bands such as Pink Floyd, Genesis, Deep Purple and Supertramp, bringing together a crowd of people interested in both the arts and pop music. Hütter and Schneider played one of their earliest Kraftwerk concerts at the club. This was less a deliberate choice, more a necessity, as the German music scene lacked an infrastructure at the time.

Another vital hotspot was located next to the Creamcheese, a gallery run by Konrad Fischer which exhibited major upcoming German artists (Sigmar Polke, for example), international artists such as Gilbert & George, as well as the latest developments in American conceptual and minimalist art. 'There was not so much musical influence, but a lot of curiosity,' Hütter remembered. 'Everything was new! The idea was to get away from the old classical situations; for us this was through happenings, or Fluxus; everything was possible.'[25]

One influence that often goes unmentioned is American pop art. Düsseldorf-based artists Polke and Gerhard Richter were developing their own German slant on US pop art. A turning point in German art history occurred with their 1963 exhibition *Capitalist Realism*. The title was an ironic jibe at a Stalinist cultural policy of 'socialist realism' and the West German consumerist ideology of the 'economic miracle'. Artist and musician Wolf Vostell also emerged from this vibrant scene. A co-founder of the Fluxus movement, alongside Nam June Paik and George Maciunas, he is considered a pioneer in video art, events and installation art.

Fluxus was an international, interdisciplinary artistic movement of the sixties and seventies that prioritized the importance of the artistic process over the finished product. The main emphasis of Fluxus was on experimental art performances which aimed at creating entirely new forms of art. Pop music hence played a crucial role, particularly in psychedelic happenings, such as Warhol's *Exploding Plastic Inevitable* events. Fluxus therefore played an important role in the fusion of the worlds of art and pop music, something that proved particularly important for Kraftwerk in the twenty-first century.

To sum up, then: German art at that time became receptive to various international influences ranging from politics and music to performance and pop art, and Düsseldorf was a real hothouse of artistic innovation. The two leading minds behind Kraftwerk were eagerly assimilating all of these influences, which would later resurface in the artistic concepts governing their musical project. Or, as Hütter summarized it: 'The idea of a holistic, non-specialized art form was in the air – from Warhol and Gilbert & George and Joseph Beuys – art as politics or social sculpture.'[26]

International Influences: Warhol and the Rest

It is important to point out that Hütter and Schneider had also, during their formative years as musicians, soaked up the international avant-garde traditions of the early twentieth century. These were the main drivers behind their specific take on retro-futurism: Kraftwerk's nostalgic longing for the futures that were never realized is an expression of their hope that artistic potentials of past avant-gardes can be recoded and made productive again in the present.

The movement most pertinent here is Italian Futurism, which foregrounded Kraftwerkian ideals such as speed and technology, and urban culture, and fetishized objects like cars and industrial machinery. In his *Manifesto del Futurismo* (*Futurist Manifesto*) (1909) the poet and art theorist Marinetti advocated a rejuvenation of the arts through a celebration of technological progress and the modernization of society.

Equally important in terms of inspiration for Kraftwerk was the pioneering composer Luigi Russolo. He developed the notion of noise as music and made a lasting impact on the avant-garde music of the twentieth century with his 1913 manifesto *L'Arte dei Rumori* (*The Art of Noises*). Notably, as a builder of experimental instruments such as his *intona-rumori* (noise-makers), Russolo may be considered a precursor to Kraftwerk's experimentation with and development of custom-built electronic instruments.

In any case, the Futurist approach of treating everyday sounds emanating from the world of labour, factories and city life as music proved hugely influential to Kraftwerk and their brand of an electronic music of noises. As Hütter commented: 'We feel a connection with Futurism and try to build upon the art forms of that period.'[27]

'Autobahn' opens with the sound of a car engine revving, followed by a honking horn – banal noises from our mundane urban environments. But it is so much more than an updated version of a Futurist 'art of noises'. In the words of art critic Michael Bracewell, the track

> was a total work – a *Gesamtkunstwerk* – its concept, vision, composition, styling, artwork, instrumentation and lyric all combining to create and intensify not just the musical presence of the song, but what the track expressed as a statement about art making in the modern world. In this sense, Kraftwerk, after 'Autobahn', became Germany's Andy Warhol: artists dedicated to expressing the quotidian landscape of a Mass Cultural age, and doing so in a manner which was itself a further expression of mass cultural technology.[28]

To make a further parallel with Warhol, the

Creamcheese club would correspond to Max's Kansas City, the preferred hang-out of the Warhol entourage, while the Kling Klang studio would be the equivalent of the Factory, where film-makers, designers, pop musicians, actors and artists would meet and collaborate. Warhol provided an important model for Kraftwerk in that he attained the position of a leading iconic artist by bridging the gap between art and popular culture.

Hütter and Schneider learned about the importance of personal image from Warhol: that is to say, the strategy of hiding the real self behind an artistic mask, stripping it of individual personality and human emotion. As Warhol famously said in 1963: 'The reason I'm painting this way is that I want to be a machine, and I feel that whatever I do and do machine-like is what I want to do.'[29] Warhol envisaged his series of identical silkscreens as his answer to the threat the technical invention of photography presented to the art of painting. By becoming a 'machine' himself, he usurped the function of the camera; he would literally 'be' a machine (instead of its 'slave' or 'master').

Hütter and Schneider, too, realized that machines would increasingly replace the work of traditional virtuoso musicians as well as that of amateurs-turned-professionals playing in pop-music bands. Their decision to be at the forefront of machine-made music meant that Kraftwerk would be able to capitalize on this development and – to a large degree – define it.

To continue the comparison, Warhol's approach of elevating everyday consumer products such as soup or soft-drinks cans, or boxes of soap into art simply by depicting them bears evident links to Kraftwerk's concept of *Alltagsmusik* (everyday music), which aimed not only to incorporate technical noises and sounds into music but also to make a new type of music that could be seen as a soundtrack to our everyday existence in the age of technology and computerization. The traffic cone on the front cover of the first two albums was an unmistakeable nod to the American artist.

The Ambivalent Concept of *Industrielle Volksmusik*

Hütter and Schneider developed a specific term to describe their musical concept: 'Our music is electronic, but we like to think of it as ethnic music from the German industrial area – *industrielle Volksmusik*. It has to do with a fascination with what we see all around us, trying to incorporate the industrial environment into our music.'[30]

Industrielle Volksmusik is a tricky expression to translate into English because it has various meanings. The literal translation of 'industrial folk music' would be misleading because the concept does not refer in any way to the two widely recognized genres of industrial and folk music.

Wolfgang Flür's explanation provides an insight into what is meant by the term *Volksmusik*: 'We wanted to create a very Germanized style of modern pop music that drew on our romantic roots and folk traditions. [. . .] All this in strong interaction with technological themes; modern instruments and our distinctive, self-conscious attitude. That was our creed.'[31] He seems to be talking about tracks such as 'Tanzmusik', 'Morgenspaziergang' or 'Franz Schubert', in which Kraftwerk re-create both Romantic melodies and the German tradition of music by (mostly) electronic means. But perhaps what is more important in this reference to the German tradition is what Kraftwerk's *industrielle Volksmusik* eschews: it is not steeped in the given American traditions of blues, jazz or rock.

'Folk music of the factories'[32] is how David Bowie summed up the concept in English. While still not a perfect rendering, it nonetheless points to what Kraftwerk mean when they use the word 'industrial'. Here's Hütter on the subject: 'It has always interested us to make industrial music. Assembly line music. Production processes, which are all around us in the industrial world.'[33] This definition links Kraftwerk's music with the musical tradition of Detroit – a city, like Düsseldorf, characterized by heavy industrialization and the creation of distinct musical styles (from Motown to techno) as artistic derivations of technological processes.[34]

'Industrial' refers to a modern civilization based on technology, manufacturing and the use of machines. This further implies an association with the modernist notion that noise can be beautiful, as explored by avant-gardists from Luigi Russolo to John Cage, and hence typifies a very contemporary musical aesthetic. Likewise, *Volksmusik* is certainly not 'folk music'. 'Popular electronic music' would be a good transposition but it lacks the odd semantic resonances the original term carries in German. This adds connotations of 'music of the people, by the people, for the people' – or, to use the more established term, simply, 'pop music'.

Industrielle Volksmusik refers to Kraftwerk's take on developing a regional musical tradition in Germany and so implies an originality which distinguishes their music from the dominant Anglo-American cultural influences that pervaded post-war Germany. But the phrase was also conceived in order to demarcate an artistic territory for electronic music that defined itself as a popular counterpart to the serious academic electronic music Karlheinz Stockhausen and other high-brow composers were exploring.

Last but not least, harking back to the democratic nature of popular music long before it became increasingly conformist and a tool for the dull behemoths of a globalized culture industry, Kraftwerk intended their *industrielle Volksmusik* to be an artistic vehicle of emancipation. The German philosopher Ernst Bloch argued that art has the potential to confront us with something that strikes us as completely new and previously inconceivable. Art can hence make the utopian tangible and concrete. As concerns Kraftwerk, their music could be seen as what Bloch called 'Konkrete Utopie' ('concrete utopia'), namely an aesthetic anticipation of a better world. Art, according to Bloch, can hence instigate or inspire political change. Kraftwerk put it more succinctly in the Spanish lyrics of 'Electric Cafe': '*Música electrónica/Arte política.*'

2. EARLY WORKS: THE KRAFTWERK STORY UNFOLDS

Hütter and Schneider in the Kling Klang studio with Emil Schult (*left*), during the *Ralf and Florian* era.

So where did it all start? The story begins in 1968 at the Akademie in Remscheid, a small town some fifty kilometres outside Düsseldorf. It was there, at a summer course in which more experienced musicians mentored up-and-coming talents that Ralf Hütter and Florian Schneider first met. Both were in their early twenties and came from wealthy upper-middle-class backgrounds. Hütter's father was a businessman from Krefeld near Düsseldorf who traded in textiles. Schneider's father was the architect Paul Schneider-Esleben, famous for buildings such as the purist steel-and-glass skyscraper that is the headquarters of steel-and-engineering company Mannesmann and the modernist Cologne/Bonn airport.

Learning to play a classical instrument was part and parcel of a proper education in the German *Bildungsbürgertum* (educated middle classes) at the time; Hütter played the piano while Schneider had learned the flute and started to study music. The two seem to have immediately realized that they not only liked each other but, more importantly, that each would gain artistically from working with the other. They were united by the idea of finding new, modern ways of musical expression beyond the classical canon. As Hütter put it: 'There was classic music, yet there was no everyday contemporary music. No language for musicians to communicate through.'[1]

Little could they have known that the creative pairing of Hütter/Schneider would one day be recognized as belonging in the same league as Lennon/McCartney or Jagger/Richards. Their first band was called Organisation. Joining up with three now-forgotten musicians, Hütter and Schneider made a record that was very much a product of its time: *Tone Float* did not attract the interest of any of the few German record labels but was released in Britain in August 1969 on RCA Victor, the fairly dreadful cover featuring a psychedelically colourful male face.

The tracks were largely improvised and free-floating, refuting the patterns of Anglo-American pop music. In this, the ambient soundscapes were a harbinger of later developments. Atonal, discordant passages met sections that were clearly musically organized. There were some similarities to contemporary releases by Pink Floyd and occasional hints of fellow German synthesizer experimentalists Popol

Vuh. In commercial terms, *Tone Float* sank without trace (if you'll excuse the pun).

However, the album did feature a couple of key Kraftwerkian elements. The back cover saw the first appearance of the orange-and-white traffic cone, initially an enigmatic item that made no apparent sense: a curious graphic detail, an everyday object often seen on German roads. More importantly, the album was produced and engineered by Konrad 'Conny' Plank and so marked the beginning of a fertile partnership that would last until *Autobahn*.

In addition, some characteristics of later Kraftwerk tracks were already discernible on the twenty-minute title track: calculated changes of tempo, melodic preferences and the interplay of repetitive percussion. After RCA dropped Organisation due to poor sales, Hütter and Schneider eventually started afresh with a new band, and that constituted the true beginning of the Kraftwerk story.

Their self-titled debut album appeared in November 1970, while Kraftwerk were still a duo. The traffic cone now took centre stage on the front cover against a white background. This was undoubtedly a Warholian strategy: imbuing a trivial object with artistic importance. In 1967, Warhol had designed a similar cover for the Velvet Underground's debut album, featuring the now-iconic banana. It marked the start of the marriage between art and pop music, a project that Hütter and Schneider pursued with dedication.

They also established their own version of Warhol's Factory, renting a dingy room in Mintropstrasse, Düsseldorf, in 1970. The name of this unassuming place, the Kling Klang studio, later also served as the name of the record label they set up.[2] 'Kling Klang' is an odd, poetic pairing. To German ears it sounds, tautologically, like something along the lines of 'resounding sound'. Like the pairing of yin and yang, the expression has something unique about it and became as iconically Kraftwerk as their music and man-machine image.

The aim was to gradually develop the Kling Klang studio into their home base and artistic fortress. The studio also represented a vital symbol of Kraftwerk's independence from the mechanisms and pressures of the music industry; it was their safe haven and a creative retreat, but also 'a key factor in the development of their music – a combination of rehearsal room, compositional tool, technological playground and, increasingly, instrumental archive',[3] as outmoded equipment was stored in the basement for potential future use.

Kraftwerk had learned a valuable lesson from their initial producer, Conny Plank: along with Can, they were among the first pop bands to recognize the studio as a musical instrument, even as a band member in its own right. It was an entirely new approach to making music, and with it came a new type of musician, one who understood himself as a synthesis of musician and sound engineer, uniting technical skills with musical expertise. Kraftwerk's work with the Kling Klang studio helped to propagate this approach, and in turn inspired producer-musicians such as Brian Eno to emulate and extend the idea.

Kraftwerk 1

The cover of *Kraftwerk*, or *Kraftwerk 1*, as it is sometimes referred to, demonstrated a complete U-turn from the design style of Organisation, solidly anchoring Kraftwerk's visual identity in modern pop art and minimalism. The traffic cone anticipated not just the traffic theme of 'Autobahn' but also the importance of movement and mobility in their work. The titles of the four instrumentals, too, indicated a considerable shift away from Organisation, whose album and track titles were in English – with *Kraftwerk 1*, Hütter and Schneider switched to their native language (even though they were not yet singing in it).

Opening track 'Ruckzuck' translates as 'right now' or 'but quickly', and this urgency is reflected in the music: dramatic changes of tempo and a driving percussive section combine to create a track that to some degree hints at what was to come in 'Trans-Europe Express'. The track title 'Megaherz' is a pun on the unit measure of frequencies named after the German physicist Heinrich Rudolf Hertz; literally, 'mega heart' in English. This elegiac piece, running close to ten minutes, is a duet between Hütter's organ and Schneider's transverse flute. It begins with a deep, rippling bass tone that steadily expands through electronic treatments to a discordant climax. There is a meditative middle section played on the flute and keyboards, and the piece closes with a series of wave-like crescendos of increasing intensity.

The closing track, 'Vom Himmel hoch' ('From Heaven Above'), references the title of a popular Christmas song, while the music mimics a wartime air raid which reanimates the horrors of civilian bombings with a minimal repertoire of percussive and electronic sounds. Together with the darkly ironic and ambivalent title, this was remarkable at the time, as the strategic bombing campaign waged against the German population during the last years of the Second World War by Allied forces was a very difficult subject to raise, particularly so for left-leaning young Germans who understood all too well that the destruction was, in a moral sense, rightful vengeance for the crimes committed by the Nazis.[4]

'Our tradition here had been broken, bombed,' Hütter said in a telling statement in 1991, pointing out that while the Nazis had destroyed the thriving modernist, avant-garde movement in Germany as soon as they came to power in 1933, the bombing campaigns by the British and US air forces had decimated German cities and infrastructure to a hitherto unimaginable degree. Aerial images of the obliteration of Cologne show the entire city as one vast field of ruins and destruction. Thousands of decomposing bodies lie buried beneath the rubble.

Speaking in 1991, Florian Schneider recalled the Düsseldorf of his childhood: 'Much of the town was still destroyed. I remember the streets were still full of bomb holes, it was a bit like it is in Lebanon now.'[5] Hütter gave a similar description in 1982: 'Our parents were bombed out of their homes. Their main interest was to reconstruct a life for themselves. They became obsessed with material things and went over the top.'[6]

The fact that Allied bombers had wiped out many urban areas of the Rhine-Ruhr area must be taken into account when considering some of Hütter's statements, such as the following, in which he aims to explain the complex situation young Germans of his generation found themselves in when trying to come to terms with their difficult national legacy: 'Germany had lost its identity. We all felt very lost.'[7] The quote implies neither nationalism nor revisionism but instead a pronounced sense of displacement and confusion in a territory that should feel familiar: one's native country.

Kraftwerk 2

Kraftwerk 2 was released in January 1972. The band were building on positive feedback in the music press: the German magazine *Sounds* had voted 'Ruckzuck' the 'song of the year', while *Kraftwerk 1* was awarded third place in its 'LP of the year' competition. More importantly, the band received the 'group of the year' accolade, over Can and Tangerine Dream. Kraftwerk's second album was very much a direct continuation of its predecessor: the cover design was replicated, now showing a traffic cone with green stripes. Their second effort still had no specific title (only a '2' stamped beneath the band name) and the titles of the eight instrumental tracks were once more in German. The decision to make the albums so similar was, again, a trick copied from Warhol. (He had issued a series of prints of the same image, the colour the only difference between them.)

The first track, which takes up nearly the entire A-side, is the seventeen-minute 'Klingklang', the result of various sound experiments undertaken by Hütter and Schneider in the studio of Ralf Arnies in Hamburg; it sounds a little like a collage of different elements merged together. For the first time, Kraftwerk used only drum machines to drive the music forward. With the constantly shifting tempo, this gave the impression that the machine was in control of the music, with the two humans simply playing along on organ and flute. No other German pop music at the time sounded anything like this.

The more atmospheric songs on the B-side don't develop into the long-form compositions that characterized the previous album but stick to a length of between three and five minutes. Exercises in minimalism, they have a child-like quality, an experimental simplicity often enhanced by the use of echo effects. Sometimes, they seem to lie unsettlingly on the verge of disintegration: drifting atmospheres perforated by isolated sounds. The track titles bear only a passing relation to the music, instead stressing the industrial image that Kraftwerk were clearly aiming to consolidate: 'Strom' ('Current'/'Electricity'), 'Spule 4' ('Reel 4') and 'Wellenklänge' ('Wave Sounds'). On the closing track, 'Harmonika' ('Harmonica'), Hütter plays repeated arpeggios on his organ.[8]

The German experimental music ensemble Zeitkratzer covered the first two Kraftwerk LPs on their two *Zeitkratzer Performs Songs from Kraftwerk and Kraftwerk 2* albums. Released in 2017 and 2019, the Zeitkratzer versions update the original tracks, but also often keep close to the Kraftwerk sound. For as long as Kraftwerk refuse to reissue their albums, the Zeitkratzer records are the best way to listen to their early material.

While working on their first few albums, Kraftwerk began earning their dues as a live band on the local and regional circuit in the Rhine-Ruhr area. Initially, some of the sets they played in galleries or arty bars stretched to six hours. Kraftwerk also appeared at small festivals as well as, from early on, on regional radio and TV shows. As the members of the band, other than the two founders, fluctuated constantly between 1970 and 1973, the sound of early live performances differed nearly every time.

The composition of the live rig or the selection of instruments to be used on stage obviously depended on the musicians playing. For half a year, while Hütter left to pursue his architectural studies, Kraftwerk lacked a keyboard, existing as a trio of Florian Schneider (flute), Klaus Dinger (drums) and Michael Rother (guitar). (Dinger and Rother were to go on to found Neu! after leaving Kraftwerk.[9])

The earliest live footage of Kraftwerk makes for odd viewing today, with the hindsight of how the band would develop. The forty-eight-minute video footage was recorded in the winter of 1970 during a concert in the small town of Soest, NRW.[10] Hütter sports a cool black leather jacket and wears his hair long, Dinger performs his prototypical, bent-over drumming-animal show, relentlessly thrashing his kit, while Schneider's work on the violin during their powerful rendition of 'Heavy Metal Kids' demonstrates – in the best John Cale fashion – that it can be a truly rock'n'roll instrument.

The set ends with an untitled improvisation, typical of their live appearances at the time, but the highlight of the gig was undoubtedly a crushing, high-speed version of 'Ruckzuck' with piercing flute stabs courtesy of Schneider and interspersed with anti-consumerist messages such as the ironic invitation 'Support the economy – celebrate Christmas more often.' The footage, which was made available by WDR TV station only in 2014, gives an unprecedented insight into very early Kraftwerk performances. It is fascinating to see how things developed from these modest beginnings to become the full-blown multimedia extravaganzas of Kraftwerk concerts today.

Kraftwerk No. 3: *Ralf and Florian*

For their third album, Kraftwerk resisted the temptation of replicating the established artwork formula. Instead of being named *Kraftwerk 3*, it was given the title *Ralf and Florian*. Under the guidance of their associate and unofficial band member Emil Schult, Hütter and Schneider manifestly began to take control of their visual image. Schult had studied art under Joseph Beuys and advised the band on conceptual ideas and their image.

Adhering to their credo that less is more, Kraftwerk have released only a relatively small number of carefully staged promo images throughout their career. The German edition of *Ralf and Florian*, issued in October 1973, was dominated by an eye-catching black-and-white portrait of the two men.[11] The pair almost seem to have been photographed in two unrelated contexts. Hütter, his hair still long, gazes enigmatically into the invisible camera, while the elegantly dressed Schneider smiles knowingly.

The decision to now openly define Kraftwerk's identity as based on the pairing of Hütter and Schneider, as well as the unusual – in a German cultural context – use of their first names, may be seen as a reference to the British artists Gilbert & George. According to David Stubbs, the duo resemble Kraftwerk in that they are 'very public and yet very private artists, for whom privacy isn't just a matter of personal temperament but a conceptual imperative'.[12] In any case, Hütter and Schneider certainly styled themselves as 'a twosome as divorced from the clichés of accepted rock presentation as one could imagine'.[13]

Gilbert & George did two Düsseldorf shows, which must have made quite an impression on Hütter and Schneider. The sharp difference between their square, quintessentially English image on the one hand and the radicalism of their artistic concepts on the other would have appealed to the core Kraftwerk team.

Crucially, both the nostalgic-ironic portrait on the front and the eerily illuminated photograph of the two musicians (taken in the Kling Klang studio) on the reverse didn't fit the visual iconography of rock music. In the latter, Hütter and Schneider look like eccentric scientists in an electronic laboratory. What gives this image its odd atmosphere is the spooky light pervading the static, artificial arrangement: the impression is of two slightly mad professors who research the otherworldly noises made by machines in an underground cavern.

Musically, the sound of *Ralf and Florian* is unmistakeably characterized by electronic instruments; unsurprisingly, as it was the first Kraftwerk album on which synthesizers were used, supplemented, once more, by a rhythm machine. Its overall sound is cleaner, and the melodies come more to the fore on the tracks that adopt the format of a song. 'Ananas Symphonie' ('Pineapple Symphony') is the first Kraftwerk track to feature, at least nominally, lyrics – the vocoderized song title is repeated several times. With the pretty 'Tanzmusik' ('Dance Music'), the album anticipated later tracks such as 'Franz Schubert': lovely faux-classical melodies played tantalizingly by electronic means.

'Tongebirge' ('Mountain of Sound') and 'Heimatklänge' ('Sounds of/from Home') are pastoral-sounding ambient tracks, prefiguring later tracks by Brian Eno. Standout track 'Kristallo', according to musician Carsten Brocker, 'reveals the adaptation of a new melodic element, and it anticipates techno by combining the drum machine with a sixteenth-note bass pattern, created by the synthesizer'.[14] The unusual title was inspired by a hotel located about a mile from the Kling Klang studio (Cristallo).

'So, there we have it – ambient, new age, classical, synth, dance music. Listening to *Ralf and Florian*'s Nostradamus-like manifesto makes for thrilling listening,'[15] Kraftwerk biographer Buckley enthuses. And rightly so. Album number 3 was a farewell to what could be called Kraftwerk's 'Era of the Traffic Cone'. The door to the future of music had been pushed open by *Ralf and Florian*, but there was still a considerable way to go – even though it didn't take Hütter and Schneider all that long to get there. *Autobahn*, their next album, was now only a small step away for Kraftwerk, but it represented a great leap forward for pop music.

As their third album attested, Kraftwerk were a unique proposition in the studio, and they were becoming increasingly so on stage. After they played their first concert outside Germany, in February 1973 at a festival near Paris, a reviewer singled them out from the other German bands appearing (such as Guru Guru, Ash Ra Tempel and Tangerine Dream): 'The group is made up of two contemplative intellectuals [. . .] from Düsseldorf. Their music is very smooth, very slick, a kind of long bewitchment [. . .] The audience was surprised at first, by the music alone, then when the lights went off and a screen appeared with luminous arabesques projected onto it, the spell was complete. [. . .] Kraftwerk are an avant-garde group who transform the electronic into the beautiful.'[16]

Hütter always stressed that early Kraftwerk, as well as Organisation, initially played at venues such as universities or galleries as part of art performances or opening events for exhibitions more out of necessity than by choice: the music infrastructure in Germany remained underdeveloped. But it was through this that Kraftwerk became very much part of the local NRW arts scene, in the same way that the Velvet Underground were instrumental to the Factory milieu in New York.

'We were lucky,' Hütter remembers. 'At the time there were happenings, the Fluxus group, etc. It was very normal, we played on the same circuit, the galleries.'[17] This fitted well with their ethos as an emerging audiovisual package, defining their appearances not so much as pop gigs but rather as the musical expression of performance artists. It was a lesson learned from Warhol, who had shown that pop culture and pop art had to transcend the dividing lines between the various art forms – the complete package is stronger than the sum of its individual components.

Such thinking in art also harks back to a very

specific German tradition, one that Hütter and Schneider were fully aware of: 'We do everything by ourselves, videos, sleeves and graphics; it's like a mosaic which leads to the productivity of Kraftwerk, but it doesn't represent one field only. In Germany, it is called *Gesamtkunstwerk*. That's what Wagner was doing in his time with theatre and music.'[18]

The term *Gesamtkunstwerk* was popularized by Richard Wagner, who intended to reunite the separate strands of the arts – music, painting, theatre and dance – in his grand opera cycle, *The Ring of the Nibelung* (1848–74). Once more, *Gesamtkunstwerk* is a specific German term that was translated variously into English: 'total artistic work', 'encompassing work of art' and 'complete artistic package' are among the more literal attempts, while 'complete audiovisual work of art' is closer to the semantic core of the concept. It's easy to see that the last definition is an apt fit for Kraftwerk's œuvre.

But Kraftwerk were not just booked by Düsseldorf galleries; they also received several offers to appear at more conventional music venues. Their varied gigging activities raised the profile of the band locally, and soon also a little further afield. Though Kraftwerk had managed to secure a handful of appearances in major cities such as Berlin and Hamburg by 1971, they mostly gigged in cities in the Rhineland region for the first half of the seventies.

It was the immense surprise success of their fourth album that took them as far as America – from speeding across the motorways of NRW to cruising the highways of the United States.

3. MOVEMENT AND VELOCITY: FROM *AUTOBAHN* TO *TRANS-EUROPE EXPRESS*

Classic Kraftwerk line-up, photographed by Maurice Seymour in New York in 1975.

'In our society, everything is in motion.
Music is a flowing art form.'

                                    – Ralf Hütter

To devote the entire A-side of your fourth album to
a twenty-three-minute track about driving a car on
a motorway might seem an odd choice. But 'Autobahn' was a perfect match of concept and music
and proved a turning point in Kraftwerk's history.
Movement and motion are at the very essence of
their music – a constant flow, an exercise in an endless momentum of sound. Many of their Krautrock
contemporaries dreamed of musical journeys into
space; the so-called *kosmische Musik* of fellow synthesizer bands such as Tangerine Dream, Ash Ra
Tempel or Popol Vuh made 'the cosmic' a metaphor
for a new spirituality – or simply an excuse to take
LSD. Kraftwerk, on the other hand, were more
sober, devoting their attention to more quotidian
methods of travel.

Ever since Goethe rambled through eighteenth-
century Italy, German culture had advocated travel
as a means to overcome the self-limitations that
result from not being able to see beyond one's own
immediate environment. As in England, the 'grand

tour' was part and parcel of the cultural fabric, but what made travelling abroad even more enlightening for Germans was leaving behind the parochialism and intellectual narrowness that came with the country's division into a patchwork of small independent states. Later, in the nineteenth and early twentieth centuries, German 'travelling' would involve the conquest of far-flung colonies and the invasion of neighbouring countries in the context of two world wars.

After the Nazi atrocities, all of that changed. Travelling beyond borders was a way for young Germans to leave behind a nationalist mindset that had dominated their parents' generation. Kraftwerk travelled a lot; to them, a genuinely German musical project entailed them simultaneously being a truly European band in their self-perception and outlook. 'We are the first German group to record in our own language, use our electronic background,' they declared, in order to 'create a Central European identity for ourselves'.[1]

Pertinent to a deeper understanding of Kraftwerk's ability to create a machine-driven music that travelled globally and spoke to different cultures is the musical journey of a beat that was culturally coded as specifically German – the motorik beat. Speakers of English may be surprised to learn that this word, derived from the English 'motoric', constitutes fantasy German; like the term 'Krautrock', it is an English invention. Motorik is the musical embodiment of momentum, the thrust of a relentless drive forward.

The group most readily identified with the motorik moniker is Neu!, the duo of former short-term Kraftwerkers Michael Rother and Klaus Dinger.[2] But the relentless ostinato rhythm of the motorik beat, which created a repetitive yet forward-flowing feel, wasn't unique to Neu!. It was also the hallmark of other German bands such as Can, driven by their drummer, Jaki Liebezeit. There is early evidence of Kraftwerk's knack for motorik in 'Ruckzuck', the opening track of their first album. Fittingly, it made a grand return in the final section of 'Autobahn' and has been a mainstay of the Kraftwerk sound ever since.

What set Kraftwerk apart from their Krautrock peers was their ability to translate this German sense of a steady, forward-thrusting rhythm into a purely electronic sound and to find fitting sonic metaphors that related the hypnotic experience of the music to a specifically German framework – driving a German car on a German *Autobahn*. The magic of Kraftwerk's music stems from this deliberate focus on relentless repetition, propelling the listener onward, emulating the velocity of travel by marrying it with the constant forward flow of beat-driven music that is the sonic equivalent of propulsion: music in perpetual motion, efficient movement and fluid motion, as showcased so very convincingly on 'Autobahn'.

'The music came from our reality. . . music of a poetic realism. . . "Autobahn" is a Kling-Klang-electro-symphony,'[3] as Hütter summed it up in 2019. It is also very much a song about German identity. '"Autobahn",' Hütter explained, 'was about finding our artistic situation: where are we? What is the sound of the German Bundesrepublik?'[4] The epic, ground-breaking song delivered a complex artistic comment on the status quo of cultural, national and musical identity in the Federal Republic in the seventies. While an Anglophone audience may most readily associate Kraftwerk with songs such as 'The Model' or 'The Robots', in Germany it's predominantly 'Autobahn' that first comes to mind whenever the band is mentioned.

The song, with its iconic chorus, is widely recognized by Germans – even though in many cases it is the only Kraftwerk song people are familiar with. 'Autobahn', in many ways, is Kraftwerk's most 'German' song. The academic Sean Albiez suggests that Kraftwerk, in attempting to define a sound that signified West Germany, 'created a soundtrack that could potentially stand in for the FRG's (Federal Republic of Germany) tainted national anthem, and that confidently represented the modernizing, rationalizing and progressive industrial intent of the emerging but fragmented nation'.[5]

Singing about the *Autobahn* network, or, to be more precise, musically emulating a car journey on the motorway, struck a chord with Germans for a number of reasons—reasons that are still relevant today. 'It's basically the musical description of a car journey from Düsseldorf to Hamburg,' claims Wolfgang Flür. 'If you know the route, you'll recognize the sounds: the mechanical sounds represent the industrial Ruhr valley, the conveyor belts of the mining towns of Bottrop and Castrop-Rauxel. Then you have the stretch through the rural Münsterland, where the countryside is symbolized by the flute and the song is completely different in feel. In short: VW and Daimler, Thyssen and Krupp, beautiful landscapes, and in between the long and winding *Autobahn*—a late classical German tale.'[6]

Driving on the *Autobahn* is deeply ingrained in the collective consciousness of the German nation: it symbolizes modernization, mobility and freedom on a motorway system with (notionally) no speed limit. Furthermore, the *Autobahn* is closely connected with car manufacturing (crucial to rebuilding the post-war economy), as well as the quality of German engineering (as captured by the Kraftwerkian marketing slogan 'Vorsprung durch Technik' ('Advancement through technology')). Most crucially, though, for many Germans, the *Autobahn*, despite being an object of national pride, inevitably conjures up its problematic origins as Hitler's prestige project.

The German motorways were originally designated as the *Straßen des Führers* (roads of the Führer), and so are a deeply ambivalent German monument, peculiarly situated between past and present, nature and technology. For a while, during their shows to promote *Autobahn* in 1975 and 1976, Kraftwerk prefaced their performances of the track 'Kometenmelodie 1' ('Comet Melody 1') from the B-side of the album with a reference to another literary monument in German culture that is deemed to be equally representative of the ambivalent trait determining the German national character: Johann Wolfgang von Goethe's great drama *Faust*.

On stage, a robotic voice declaimed four lines from the 'Prologue in Heaven', spoken by the archangel Raphael:

Die Sonne tönt nach alter Weise,
In Brudersphären Wettgesang,

Und ihre vorgeschrieb'ne Reise
Vollendet sie mit Donnergang.

(The Sun sings out, in ancient mode,
His note among his brother-spheres,
And ends his pre-determined road
With peals of thunder for our ears.)

On a superficial level, this poetic description of
the sun running its daily course from dusk to dawn
sets the scene for the spectacle of the comets to be
seen in the night sky (as musically evoked in the
'Kometenmelodie' suite). However, many Germans
recognize these lines as belonging to the 1808 drama
that has come to be widely seen as an allegory of the
German tragedy of the early twentieth century: the
story of the scientist Faust who sold his soul to the
devil in return for the power of knowledge and eventually has to face the horrible consequences. The
folk story echoed the fate of the German people,
who had sold their souls to the political seducer
Hitler, hoping he would make the nation strong
again – and then had to face the consequences of a
lost war, a destroyed country and disgrace in the eyes
of the world.

The overtly electronic soundscape of *Autobahn*,
as well as the title song's radio-unfriendly duration of
nearly twenty-three minutes, challenged the norms

of standardized rock music. Arriving some twenty years after the popular birth of rock'n'roll (if one is inclined to treat the release of Elvis's debut album from 1956 as marking this momentous event), Kraftwerk gave listeners an idea about what the future would sound like – music made by machines, a novel form of pop music without drums and guitars, featuring synthetic robot voices enunciating the lyrics.

The format of the pop song, with its verse/chorus structure, is replaced by an electronic composition running for the duration of the side of a vinyl album. It goes almost without saying that 'Autobahn' ends after twenty-two minutes and forty-three seconds only because of the limitations of the vinyl record format; the impetus of this track obviously stretches beyond this, ideally for a few hours, to truly simulate a drive on the *Autobahn*.

'The Autobahn Goes on Forever', claims the title of a seminal article by the music journalist Chris Bohn. As he points out, what made 'Autobahn' such a particular challenge to English-language rock was the fact that the Germans inadvertently beat it at its own game, given the central place that the mythology of the road occupied, particularly in America. From Canned Heat's 'On the Road Again' to Steppenwolf's 'Born to be Wild' and Bruce Springsteen's 'Born to Run', 'Autobahn', according to Bohn, 'has superseded Route 66 in the roadmap of rock history'.[7]

'Autobahn' also proved to be a personal landmark for Kraftwerk. As they admitted in an interview in 1975, 'we often had the dream of hearing our music on the radio one day [. . .] and with "Autobahn" it became a reality. When we were touring America, we suddenly heard ourselves.'[8] This watershed moment (supposedly) happened when the band were on their way from the airport to their hotel: in a stupendous act of life imitating art, their actual experience in the car is mimicked by the section of their song when the car stereo is switched on.

The version they heard was a radio-friendly three-and-a-half-minute mix. After 'Autobahn', which to many sounded as if it had fallen out of the future, was first played on the radio in full by a Chicago radio station, Kraftwerk's American manager, Ira Blacker, commissioned an edit for the single, knowing that the track would have to be this length in order to secure entry into the US charts. And it worked: the single climbed up to number 25 in the Billboard charts and this kick-started sales of the album, which peaked at number 5 and stayed in the charts for more than four months.

It was Blacker, too, who secured Kraftwerk's legendary record deal, which guaranteed them unprecedented artistic freedom and aesthetic sovereignty. This advantageous contract allowed Kraftwerk to retain ownership of all their recorded work and to manage their own recording deadlines. Being essentially a licensing agreement, it allowed them to keep control over their business affairs. This arrangement gave Kraftwerk the freedom to work in the Kling Klang studio without outside interference and to release records if and when they wanted to – a freedom they have made ample use of ever since, with intervals between albums on occasion being over a decade. 'We have a Buddhist technique to stay patient,'[9] Hütter once remarked – and he probably wasn't joking.

Although Kraftwerk wasn't the only German band playing electronic music to enjoy recognition in the US – Tangerine Dream were doing surprisingly well there, too – no other band could match the chart success and media interest that surrounded the four-piece from Düsseldorf. 'Kraftwerk Electrify America', ran the headline of a report in teen mag *Bravo* in the summer of 1975. 'Hopefully, we will now also find more fans at home in Germany. That would really delight us most,' Hütter told the reporter.

But the triumphant run of the US tour also raised suspicion of a 'German invasion'. For example, Lester Bangs (in)famously asked in his notorious 'Kraftwerkfeature'[10] in *Creem* in September 1975: 'Where is rock going?', only to provide the answer himself: 'It's being taken over by the Germans and the machines.' *Autobahn*, to him, was 'more than just a record, it is an *indictment*. An indictment of all those who would resist the bloodless iron will and order of the ineluctable dawn of the Machine Age.'[11]

His interview-essay is indicative of many of the stupid Nazi clichés that Kraftwerk had to deal with in English-speaking countries. Florian Schneider, Bangs claimed, looks 'like he could build a computer or push a button and blow up half the world with the same amount of emotion'.[12] Hütter and Schneider decided to react to the insulting stereotypes by retorting in kind: rather than critically responding, they ironically exaggerated and coldly satirized Anglo-American truisms about Germans by assuming the roles assigned to them: 'We want the whole world to know our background. We cannot deny we are from Germany, because the German mentality, which is more advanced, will always be part of our behaviour.'[13]

Stupid stereotypes, indeed. But by playing the role of cold Germans openly flirting with Nazism, Kraftwerk had also delivered a perfect performance off stage: they smartly seized the opportunity to forge an identity and image that set them apart from any competitor. 'In the grand self-mythologizing world of American rock, they had outmanoeuvred every major act on the scene by projecting a revolutionary image which had laid the groundwork for how they would be perceived from this point on,' wrote Tim Barr.[14]

Nevertheless, this was a dangerous strategy, and they may have regretted it once they saw the piece in print. The article was emblazoned with an illustration showing a Nazi-style eagle holding a large swastika in its claws, which made the piece look as if it were an official Nazi propaganda publication from the thirties. One particularly hideous attempt by Bangs to steer Kraftwerk towards Nazi imagery was his suggestion that electrodes should be implanted into the brains of their audience, allowing the band to communicate this way:

> 'Yes,' enthused Ralf, 'this would be fantastic.' The final solution to the music problem, I suggest.
> 'No, not the solution. The next step.'[15]

The British media, typically, picked up on this section. The *NME*'s reprint of the article unashamedly blurted out: 'Kraftwerk: the final solution to the Music Problem?'. Encouraged by *Creem*'s choice of illustration, the *NME* interview was accompanied by a photo of the band inserted into an image of the

Party Convention Grounds in Nuremberg, insinuating once more that Kraftwerk were bona fide Nazis. How insulting this was to Germans who were adamant anti-fascists need not be stressed. The very act of reclaiming the *Autobahn* was intended as a way to break with the Nazi past. However, by playing to and toying with the prevalent clichés in the English-speaking world, Kraftwerk did invite such treatment.

The reason Kraftwerk needed to raise their profile with an Anglophone audience was linked to the fact that, in Germany, 'Autobahn' was largely met with apathy on its release in November 1974. One explanation for this could be that it was so avant-garde many people didn't know what to think about it. Here was a trail-blazing composition lasting more than twenty minutes, an experimental soundscape that included sound effects of car horns, radio static, engine noise, Doppler effects and the like, indebted to *musique concrète* yet at the same time a novelty song with child-like lyrics, and as such misunderstood by many to be a satire of the mainstream *Schlager* genre.

American music journals, however, were quick to spot the innovative quality of *Autobahn*, which was initially only available on import. This may have been due to the fact that, to American ears, this odd music seemed to come literally out of nowhere. Or perhaps it had to do with the fact that Americans could readily relate to a song that celebrated long road journeys. In any case, teen magazine *Circus* dubbed Kraftwerk 'one of the most important new acts this year';[16] *Billboard* described the album as a 'fascinating mix of guitars, percussion, strings and electronics';[17] and *Cash Box* praised the 'dynamic new sound made up of some tremendously catchy themes. [. . .] The quartet is pushing new frontiers, we look [forward to them becoming] a significant part of progressive music.'[18]

Compare this to the reception of the album in Germany: though there is a fair chance that underground, small-print-run magazines took note of the album, as far as the mainstream music press was concerned, this earthquake in the history of German pop music (and beyond) went unnoticed. Only one short review was published at the time of its release, in the November 1974 issue of the magazine *Sounds*. The reviewer liked the record and showed a familiarity with Kraftwerk's previous records. 'Autobahn' is favourably described as a 'varied, and above all entertaining jaunt which particularly impresses listeners wearing headphones'.[19]

But that was it. No excitement about the arrival of something utterly new. No overall appreciation of the album as a masterpiece, a musical milestone or at least an important step for German music. A new era had started, but neither the reviewer nor the vast majority of German music experts or listeners seemed to have noticed – at least not immediately.

After some time, reviewers did begin to take notice of the album, though not necessarily favourably. Quite a few German music critics were violently opposed to the 'decidedly clichéd rhythm structures' on *Autobahn* or dismissed the album in their reviews of later Kraftwerk releases: 'Something like that doesn't even deserve to be released.'[20]

A bone of contention in Germany which, for obvious reasons, did not play any role in the Anglophone perception of 'Autobahn' was the lyrics. They were seen as trivial, or childish, and it was probably for this reason that even today literary critics fail to detect their subtext, belittling them as nursery rhymes or for their comic-book simplicity. It appears that – perhaps because pop music is perceived as a trivial genre – it was inconceivable to some listeners that the (deceptively) simple song texts were more complex than they appeared at first glance.

A similar line of thinking is evident in the attitude many critics took towards the vocoderized voice at the beginning of the track. This effect was seen purely as the hallmark of a novelty song. In fact, electronically treating the human voice in a song was one of the most revolutionary moves in the history of pop music, as the hundreds of chart hits since testify.

The central line, 'Wir fahr'n fahr'n fahr'n auf der Autobahn' ('We drive drive drive on the motorway'), led some English speakers to believe it was a deliberate reference to The Beach Boys' 'Fun Fun Fun' – the all-American paean to cruising around in a T-bird. But the phonetic similarity was probably just a coincidence.

Vor uns liegt ein weites Tal
Die Sonne scheint mit Glitzerstrahl
Die Fahrbahn ist ein graues Band
Weiße Streifen, grüner Rand.

(Ahead of us a valley wide
The sun shines with sparkling light
The lane is a grey concrete strip
White stripes, green ditch.)

Such lines celebrated the combination of nature and technology, claiming an aesthetic value for something that could easily be dismissed as mundane. That alone was quite a provocation for a German audience. Not only had the Nazis celebrated their *Autobahn* project in the same way, as a very modern unity of roads and landscapes, Kraftwerk's words lacked any critical component regarding the ecological issues being discussed in Germany at the time: namely, the introduction of speed limits to reduce traffic fatalities and exhaust emissions, and the ongoing question of fossil-fuel resources.

The international oil crisis in 1973, the year before the album's release, caused record highs in fuel prices due to petrol shortages and people were banned from using private motor vehicles on Sundays for a month. Newspapers printed eerie pictures of motorways without any cars on them. Accordingly, people literally took to the streets, taking Sunday strolls on the deserted *Autobahn*. (The peaceful 'Morgenspaziergang' ('Morning Stroll') on the B-side of the album may be an allusion to this odd episode in German motoring history.)

Similarly, the cover image of the German edition showed a highly idealized scene of a long stretch of an *Autobahn* but with only two cars on it – a black Mercedes driving towards the onlooker and a white Volkswagen Beetle driving away. This seemingly simple tableau is full of hidden references to German history that beg to be deciphered.

For instance, one could interpret the VW Beetle (Hütter owned one at the time) seen driving towards the sunrise on the horizon as symbolizing the hopes of Kraftwerk's generation for a brighter future beyond the troubled Nazi past. After all, the black Mercedes (a make of car used by political leaders such as Adolf Hitler and West Germany's first chancellor, Konrad Adenauer) is shown driving in the opposite direction. It is, one could say, driving back to the past, to where it belongs.

In addition, the concrete strip isn't the only sign of civilization that interrupts the natural landscape; the poles of a powerline run horizontally through the image – a self-referential visual clue to the band's name, carrying the electricity generated in a power plant and used by Kraftwerk to make electronic music. And the 'Wir' ('We') in the lyrics doesn't refer just to the band or describe a specific journey on the *Autobahn* – it could equally well refer to German listeners singing along with the lyrics; they, too, will perceive trips on a motorway as part of their everyday life. The lyrics also need to be understood as an attempt to construct a national, sonic community.

The plans for a national motorway network had already been developed before the Nazis came to power, but they seized their chance and immediately started to accelerate the *Reichsautobahn* project. The propagandistic role of the *Autobahn* was to promise a bright future of technological progress and affordable mobility for all Germans. That very promise, however, materialized only after the war for West Germans. Increasing mobility as a major indicator of the modernization of Germany society, although it began with Hitler's former pet project, the *Kraft-durch-Freude-Wagen*, a.k.a. Volkswagen, and its corollary, the *Autobahn*, was in itself proof that German society was making palpable progress away from its horrendous past.

The lyrics of 'Autobahn' are, of course, a direct, accurate image description of the cover illustration – both were created by long-term collaborator Emil Schult. *Autobahn* was Kraftwerk's first stab at a concept album: music, words and image form a close-knit artistic package. Today, the iconic image truly comes alive in the visuals for the live performances of 'Autobahn', where animated cars can be seen speeding up and down the motorway. When Hütter was asked in 2017 if, after nearly forty-five years, he was not bored at still having to play 'Autobahn', he responded in the negative. With a nod to the coffee cup in front of him, he pointed out that if things are very good, you don't tire of them.[21]

With their breakthrough track, Kraftwerk indelibly changed the perception of the *Autobahn*, and not just in Germany. 'Autobahn' took German pop music to a new level, marrying avant-gardism and the conceptual with pop sensibilities. Hütter and Schneider must have realized their achievement themselves, as the short instrumentals on the B-side – interesting as they are on their own terms – cannot compete with the A-side title track and can feel like little more than fillers.

The fact that 'Autobahn' still 'works' to this day is testament to the timeless qualities of the song: once you have heard 'Autobahn', it becomes impossible to take a ride on the motorway without the tune coming to mind. (Even if only as a light-hearted sing-along to entertain the children.) Asked about David Bowie's visits to see Kraftwerk, Hütter stated: 'When he came to see us in Düsseldorf in his Mercedes, he took the highway while listening to "Autobahn" on the car stereo. He said: it's exactly like that, everything is in your tune.'[22]

The Triumphant US Tour

Kraftwerk's first tour, in early 1975, took them all the way from Düsseldorf to America, to play in the hallowed homeland of rock in the wake of 'Autobahn''s surprise success in the States. Working on their image prior to the tour, Hütter and Schneider decided that, conforming to convention, Kraftwerk should consist of four band members.

Wolfgang Flür had been recruited in October 1973 and made his first appearance on the TV culture programme *Aspekte*, broadcast in the same month.

There, he showcased a self-built electronic drum kit – a crude, improvised-looking apparatus that was completed only a few days before the TV recording, it had dozens of wires emerging from the back and a crude silver-foil cover for the casing. Yet what several hundred thousand TV viewers were seeing was something completely new and totally beyond any conception of a pop-music instrument. With what appeared to be knitting needles, Flür was 'drumming' on twelve round metal plates (which had been salvaged from a scrapyard). The TV appearance, in which both Hütter and Schneider seem very nervous, drew a lot of publicity.

Preparing for their tour of the United States, the core team felt that Kraftwerk needed another electronic 'drummer' and asked Karl Bartos to join, thus bringing the headcount to four. Bartos was a trained classical musician who had studied percussion at the Robert Schumann Conservatory in Düsseldorf, making him the ideal addition to complete the Kraftwerk 'rhythm section'. Finally, the group had found the line-up that would be responsible for the great albums from *Radio-Activity* to *Techno Pop*.

The US tour took the four-piece to some forty cities. The exact number of concerts is not known, as the twenty-two-date tour originally planned was constantly extended by further bookings once

Kraftwerk were on American soil. The tour also included a high-profile performance of 'Autobahn' on the TV show *Midnight Special* on 25 July 1975. Live, Kraftwerk played a version of their chart hit that could run for up to forty minutes (nearly doubling the studio version), as well as other, shorter tracks from the B-side and a selection from their first three albums. Set opener 'Ruckzuck' was markedly different from the studio version, notably because the two live percussionists added more weight to the music and more drive to the sound.

The tour of the United States was followed by a seventeen-date tour of the United Kingdom in September 1975. The article that drew parallels between the band and the Nazis had by then appeared in the *NME* and its repercussions were clearly felt in poor ticket sales, as Karl Bartos recalls: 'We played in mostly empty halls in Newcastle, London, Bournemouth, Bath, Cardiff, Birmingham and finally in Liverpool.'[23]

Further European dates to promote *Radio-Activity* took Kraftwerk across the Netherlands, Denmark, Belgium, France and Switzerland in 1976, topped off with three more gigs in England that autumn. This very busy period of touring concluded on 10 October 1976 at the Roundhouse, London. After this appearance, Kraftwerk retreated to the

Kling Klang studio. They did not play another concert for half a decade.

More than the average rock band, Kraftwerk relied on having complex, fully functional equipment at their disposal. Their entire show depended on the electronic instrumentation working properly, even under difficult conditions and the varying technical standards in each country. Hütter explained: 'I remember that we played Paris on 110 volts and all the tempos were out of tune. At 8 p.m. the big factories that plug into the mains network were making the voltage fluctuate. That's the reality, Peugeot were making our tempos change.'[24]

Bartos recalls a near-disaster at the Paris gig during their tour of France: 'We played in Lille, in Lyon and in the famous Olympia in Paris. Not a bad show, if I remember correctly. But shortly before the start of the show, my electronic drums broke down and failed to make the slightest sound. Peter Bollig, our assistant, appeared with a soldering iron on stage – at the time we had no curtain – and soldered calmly away to repair the kit.'[25]

Touring with fickle electronic equipment was a nerve-racking business, fraught with both logistical and technical problems This was compounded by Florian Schneider's stage fright and his dislike of being without his creature comforts while on tour.

Clearly, he felt more at ease in the studio, pottering around with his speech-synthesis equipment. Over the years to come, his erratic behaviour and occasional reluctance to go on stage would cause stressful scenes in the Kraftwerk camp.

At a gig in Melbourne in 1981 Schneider escaped from the backstage area and sat in the front row to await the beginning of the concert. He was spotted through the stage curtain by Emil Schult, who managed to persuade him to join the rest of the band on stage for the concert, threatening that if he did not comply, both the tour and the band would come to an immediate end. It was only then that Schneider relented.

Radio-Activity

> 'It was like our dedication to the age of radio and radiation at the same time, breaking the taboo of including everyday political themes in the music.'
>
> – Ralf Hütter

Kraftwerk have always been reluctant to discuss their work; it's part of a larger strategy to obscure the meaning of what they do. They have always preferred to amplify the contradictions and tensions that spring from their artistic output rather than seeking to resolve them. In a further evasive move, they also like to pretend that everything is so self-explanatory it requires no comment: 'You don't have to explain it, I think that the things speak for themselves,' Schneider maintained. 'That's one reason why I don't like to explain so much what we do.'[26]

Yet the many contradictions evoked by their work continue to puzzle: men or machines, German or European, futurist or nostalgic, or all of these seeming oppositions at the same time? We are constantly forced to grapple with the incongruities the band presents. The ambivalence in their work raises questions that are not resolved, inviting the listener to come to grips with what is presented on their own.

Consider, for example, the innocuous 'Morgenspaziergang' ('Morning Stroll') from the B-side of *Autobahn*. It 'combines electronic beeps with a simple melody played on a recorder to indicate a conflict between tradition and modernity that became part of Kraftwerk's appeal'.[27] 'Radio Stars' (from *Radio-Activity*) could be assumed to refer to successful musical entertainers known through being broadcast on air but, as the lyrics reveal, it is in fact about the astronomical phenomenon of pulsars and quasars (stars that emit electromagnetic radio waves).

Or take 'Neon Lights' from *The Man-Machine*: a beguiling song about the many commercial neon lights that illuminated the streets of Düsseldorf in the mid-seventies. Invented in the first decade of the twentieth century, they were popular from the twenties until well into the sixties. When the song is performed live today, the nostalgic visuals show a long succession of neon signs advertising brands, fashion shops, bars and nightclubs that have long since disappeared. As have, of course, neon lights as a way of advertising.

Today, massive LCD advertising displays showing animated images in high resolution can be found in city centres and along arterial roads. The contrast to the old flickering neon signs is stark. Ironically, Kraftwerk now also use the newest video projection technology for the giant display of their 3D visuals at live appearances. When playing 'Neon Lights', the result is as contradictory as it gets: cutting-edge digital 3D technology is used to create a nostalgic reminder of products of a bygone era.

Nowhere is the band's strategy of ambivalence as pronounced as on *Radio-Activity*, the speedy successor to *Autobahn*, released in 1975. The oscillation between radio broadcasting and nuclear radiation – both are 'in the air for you and me' – is already encapsulated by the hyphen separating the two nouns of the album title. The bilingual lyrics of the title song are equally ambiguous:

Radioactivity
Is in the air for you and me
Radioactivity
Discovered by Madame Curie
Radioactivity
Tune in to the melody
Radioaktivität
Für dich und mich in All entsteht
  [originates in space for you and me]
Radioaktivität
Strahlt Wellen zum Empfangsgerät
  [radiates waves to the receiver]
Radioaktivität
Wenn's um unsere Zukunft geht
  [because/when our future is at stake]

The final line in German has to be understood as a comment on contemporary debates on nuclear energy. Yet it remains unclear if the song perceives nuclear energy as a positive opportunity or a negative development: is it a clean alternative to the limited supply of fossil fuels or an irresponsible threat to the environment? Neither song nor album, provides a clue. And this, unbeknown to Kraftwerk, would soon reveal itself as a risky gambit.

In Germany in the seventies there was mounting political resistance to the expansion of nuclear energy. When the construction of a nuclear power plant was approved in the small south-western settlement of Wyhl in February 1975, local protesters, from farmers to students, occupied the site until they were forcefully removed by the police. Increasing political pressure on the regional government created adverse publicity. Eventually, the licence was withdrawn by the ruling of an administrative court.

The plant was never built, and the land became a nature reserve. This successful outcome fuelled further protest against the construction of plants in other areas. In 1976 and 1977 mass demonstrations took place in the small towns of Kalkar, on the river Rhine near the Dutch border, and at Brokdorf, just north of Hamburg. This time, however, the building of the plants was violently enforced by the state with the help of thousands of riot and border police.

In February 1977 one of the largest political protests then seen in Germany took place in Brokdorf, with over 100,000 activists taking to the streets to show their opposition to nuclear energy. This and other protests which were staged at regular intervals were forcefully squashed by the authorities with the help of roadblocks, stop-and-search measures, water cannons and armoured cars. State power proved overwhelming and the completed Brokdorf nuclear power reactor started operation in October 1986.

Given the public hostility to nuclear energy, it wasn't necessarily a clever move by Kraftwerk to follow the wishes of their record company: promo shots for *Radio-Activity* were taken at a Dutch nuclear power plant. The band members wore white lab coats and looked jolly, and these images seemed to signal their approval of nuclear energy. As David Stubbs writes, 'Kraftwerk were inclining towards a bland endorsement of nuclear energy,'[28] but they did so only to provoke the hippies and to give themselves a modernistic, technology-oriented image. Whether they actually supported nuclear energy was a different matter. In a way, the name of their band placed them in a dilemma: to condemn a modern technology for generating electricity would undermine their image.

Unsurprisingly, many listeners wrongly held the entire album to be a paean to nuclear energy – despite the fact that it was inspired by the band's tour of the United States to promote *Autobahn*. At the time, *Billboard* magazine featured the most-played singles by the large network of radio stations under the heading 'Radio Action'. The band seemed to have misread or misremembered this as 'Radio-Activity'. 'Suddenly,' remembers Wolfgang Flür, 'there was a theme in the air, the activity of radio stations, and the title of "Radioactivity is in the Air for You and Me" was born. All we needed was the music to go with it. [. . .] The ambiguity of the theme didn't come until later.'[29]

Radio-Activity was intended to celebrate radio broadcasting as a convenient, easy and democratic means to listen to music and news. In the seventies, radio was of course still the prime medium for music. Numerous pop songs celebrate the radio. Just think of Charlie Dore's 'Pilot of the Airwaves' (1979), in which a radio DJ becomes a distant companion to the lonely singer. Queen had a hit with 'Radio Ga Ga' in 1984 and REM with 'Radio Song' in 1991. One of the greatest songs about the radio is surely Joy Division's 'Transmission'. According to Greil Marcus, it is 'a dramatization of the realization that the act of listening to the radio is a suicidal gesture. It will kill your mind. It will rob your soul.'[30]

In 'Autobahn', Kraftwerk had already made a flippant reference to the car radio as a source of entertainment on long car journeys:

Jetzt schalten wir das Radio an
Aus dem Lautsprecher klingt es dann:

'Wir fahr'n fahr'n fahr'n auf der Autobahn.'

(Now we switch the radio on
And from the speakers it sounds:
'We drive drive drive on the motorway.)'

The striking album artwork devised by Schult depicted an outdated radio receiver. It immediately suggested a tension between obsolete technology and the avant-garde music heard on the record. More importantly, it referenced the Nazi past through the image's strong resemblance to the DKE 38 model *Volksempfänger* (people's receiver) utilized by the Nazis to deliver their propaganda programmes to German homes. Clearly, from a German perspective, the radio represented no innocent medium – like the internet in today's world, it could be used for both political manipulation and to open minds by acquainting listeners with avant-garde music.

On the track 'News', Kraftwerk explore the radio as a medium of information. The overlaid voices of several German presenters can be heard announcing news regarding the future of nuclear energy (the plan to erect fifty new nuclear power plants in Germany can be distinguished in the polyphony of voices). The voice collage does, however, also mention the danger of limited supplies of uranium, given the intention by the nuclear lobby to build more than two thousand nuclear reactors by the year 2000.

But apart from this proviso, the news snippets selected for 'News' cannot be said to cast a critical light on nuclear energy. Once more, Kraftwerk did not side with the protest movement but remained neutral. Looked at from today's perspective, 'News' exposes the exaggerated expectations of the nuclear lobby. The envisaged number of nuclear plants was never remotely attained: today, there are about 450 reactors in operation worldwide, eight of them located in Germany.

The anti-nuclear protests remained one of the strongest political issues in West Germany in the wake of the album's release. The Green Party was founded in 1980 and began to thrive politically, feeding on the widespread public interest in ecological issues. Given this political atmosphere, Kraftwerk must have rapidly come to regret their ambivalent stance towards nuclear energy. In 1981, they adapted the lyrics of the song when they performed it live and positioned themselves on the side of the protest movement. The song now unmistakeably demanded: 'Stop radioactivity!' It remains a unique modification of the Kraftwerk œuvre. And it did not stop at that.

When, in April 1986, the Chernobyl nuclear reactor in the Soviet Union exploded, large swathes of radioactive particles were carried across to Germany. The disaster delivered undisputable proof that nuclear power plants posed a global threat, with no regard to national borders or political systems. Unsurprisingly, anti-nuclear sentiment gained further traction in Germany, and when a re-recording of 'Radioactivity' was released in 1991 on *The Mix*, Kraftwerk showcased the anti-nuclear lyrics on the updated recording, too.

Further changes were implemented. The final line of the German lyrics now ran: '*Weil's um unsere Zukunft geht*' ('Because it concerns our future'). The band also added a new introduction that made reference to sites of nuclear accidents: as well as Chernobyl, the list included Harrisburg, Sellafield and, significantly, Hiroshima, in order to make a political statement that the nuclear power lobby and the military-industrial complex in the US (and elsewhere) were close allies.

With two new lines, 'Chain reaction and mutation/Contaminated population', there was now no doubt left that Kraftwerk were lending their support to the anti-nuclear movement. They also took part in an anti-nuclear benefit show in Manchester in

June 1992 which was headlined by U2. Organized by Greenpeace, the event sought to raise the profile of the protest against the building of a second nuclear facility at Sellafield in Cumbria. The atomic power station formerly known as Windscale had been the site of a number of potentially dangerous accidents and was under criticism because there was a high incidence of cancer among the local population.

Later, Kraftwerk added even greater weight to their anti-nuclear message by using a new introduction on stage in which a robot voice declared:

Sellafield 2 will produce 7.5 tons of
   plutonium every year
1.5 kilogram of plutonium makes a nuclear bomb
Sellafield 2 will release the same amount of
   radioactivity
Into the environment as Chernobyl every
   4.5 years
One of these radioactive substances,
Krypton 85, will cause death and skin cancer

This political partisanship was a highly unusual step for a group that placed a great deal more importance on their art than on their politics. The profound ambivalence that had so strongly characterized *Radio-Activity* was sacrificed. Some fans may have wished that Kraftwerk had remained true to their concept and stayed apolitical. But Hütter and Schneider must have concluded that the political cause was worth this move. In the same way that some cycle enthusiasts consider 'Tour de France' the ultimate theme tune for their sport, Kraftwerk could be described as the 'musical wing' of the anti-nuclear movement from the early eighties on.

The irresponsible management of nuclear energy came once more to light in March 2011 when a tsunami hit the power plant located in the Japanese city of Fukushima. Kraftwerk now dropped the intro referring to Sellafield and added Fukushima to the list of disasters in what amounts to their third version of 'Radioactivity'. Their first performance of it was in July 2012, at the No Nukes protest rally held close to Tokyo and organized by Japanese musician Ryuichi Sakamoto, leader of the Yellow Magic Orchestra (whose synth-pop was strongly influenced by Kraftwerk). Kraftwerk had also added new lines in Japanese, which translate as: 'Now also in Japan/ Radioactivity today forever/Fukushima radioactivity/Air, water, all contaminated/Immediately stop'.

In its current live incarnation, 'Radioactivity' is an indisputable highlight of every Kraftwerk concert, presenting a sonic cocktail of shrill beeps, deep bass beats and a catchy melody against a background of striking visuals. At the same time, it delivers a strong political message that reflects the weight of the political reaction in Germany to the Fukushima disaster.

The incident was seen as proof of the seemingly dormant dangers of nuclear energy and caused the conservative government under Chancellor Angela Merkel to make a surprising U-turn in her party's long-standing support for nuclear power. Yet while Kraftwerk must be commended for lending their support to a worthwhile political cause, in purely artistic terms, they compromised their original vision.

The issues surrounding the band's stance towards nuclear energy tend to obscure the artistic achievements of their fifth album, which was a great leap forward for Kraftwerk. *Radio-Activity* was their first concept album proper (on *Autobahn*, the B-side did not align with the motorway theme) and also their first entirely electronic album ('Autobahn' featured small amounts of flute and guitar).

Only with their fifth album did Kraftwerk truly become an electro-pop act. *Radio-Activity* was also issued with an English-language cover (while the music remained the same); all subsequent Kraftwerk albums from *Trans-Europe Express* up to *The Mix* were released in a parallel version with English lyrics for the international market. (*Radio-Activity* was particularly successful in France, where it reached the top of the album charts; in Germany, the record made it only to number 22 and it failed to make the top 100 in America.)

But is it fair to call *Radio-Activity* an album at all? It could be said that it emulates rather a radio programme consisting of music and spoken word. It delivers an integrated sound collage of noises, interference and static, instrumental passages, spoken word, alluring melodies and catchy pop songs. In its experimental nature, it paved the way for later developments in the wider area of radio drama; experiments with the format of the radio play at the interface of auditory media art and pop music today occupy a special place in German culture.[31]

Radio-Activity was not just an album about the present and the future, but also an album about the past, because of its strong autobiographical roots: Hütter and Schneider had created a homage to the magic that radio possessed during their childhoods. In an interview conducted in 1976, Hütter explained:

We always listened to this programme called 'Nachtmusik' ['Night Music'] when we were little. That's our background, it is how we were inspired to form a purely electronic group [. . .] When it was dark and we had to go to bed, we would listen to 'Nachtmusik' under the pillow with a transistor radio. [. . .] Radio has always fascinated us deeply. We saw ourselves, Kraftwerk, in the Kling Klang studio, to be a kind of radio station of our own.[32]

This profound debt to nightly radio programmes playing experimental electronic music is evidenced by the gloomy mood piece 'The Voice of Energy'. Against a background of electrostatic crackling, a disembodied voice issues the following warning:

This is the Voice of Energy
I am a giant electrical generator
I supply you with light and power
And I enable you to receive speech
Music and images through the ether.
I am your servant and lord at the same time
Therefore, guard me well
Me, the Genius of Energy.

This track could be described as Kraftwerk's only cover version: it is a straightforward remake of a speech-synthesis experiment undertaken by Werner Meyer-Eppler in 1949, one that would probably have been featured on the nightly broadcasts by WDR. The artificial voice must have left a lasting impression on the young Florian Schneider, who later, with Kraftwerk, undertook truly pioneering work in the use of phonetic experiments in pop music. In *Radio-Activity*, there are several instances where Schneider's voice treatments create deeply eerie and weird moments, such as in the ninety seconds of 'Uranium', which deals with radioactive decay.

The elegiac 'Ohm Sweet Ohm' would provide perfect funeral music, were it not for the optimistic turn it takes towards the end of the track, where the deeply mournful melody speeds up and becomes sincerely uplifting. Indeed, it is the genius of Kraftwerk to unite apparent opposites in *Radio-Activity*. 'Airwaves' marries the sensibilities of a pop tune to the sonic experiments Karlheinz Stockhausen undertook in his early electronic composition *Studies I & II* (1953/54).

Hütter and Schneider translated Stockhausen's groundbreaking approaches to composition and electronic music into the musical grammar of pop. What often sounded harsh, abstract and elitist when utilized by the composer was transformed into avant-gardist yet alluring pop music by the band. Kraftwerk and Stockhausen had realized the revolutionary new aspect of electronic music. Stockhausen stated that 'music now cannot only be sung or played on traditional instruments but it is also possible to produce one's own sounds for a new piece. And you know how certain sounds are formed. That opens up a completely new horizon for the whole of Western music.'[33]

Kraftwerk also shared Stockhausen's idea 'not only to create a new language for music but also to encourage new ways of listening to it'.[34] On *Radio-Activity* they clearly suggested a new way of listening to music by releasing an album that merged pop sensibilities with avant-garde experimentation. And the perfect vehicle for such an undertaking was indeed the theme of radio: returning to their childhood memories of secretly listening to 'a lot of late night programmes with strange sounds and noise'[35] and making it clear that listening to 'it was part of our upbringing, our education. We always considered ourselves the second generation of electronic explorers, after Stockhausen.'[36]

Trans-Europe Express:
Futurist Nostalgia

What a contradiction! *Trans-Europe Express* came out in 1977, at the apex of the punk explosion. Yet the cover artwork sees the band posing in a way that was completely at odds with the anarchic spirit of the times. The nostalgic – you could almost say kitsch – image was taken in 1975 by New York photographer Maurice Seymour in the style typical of forties or fifties celebrity portraits in which his studio specialized. Dressed conservatively in suits, the four Kraftwerkers give a conformist, highly conventional impression; based on the photograph, one would assume they were a string quartet or a group of junior bankers. The only note of irony in this conservative look is the rhinestone brooch in the form of a musical note worn by Schneider.[37]

This out-of-date and traditionalist imagery stood in contrast to the music on *Trans-Europe Express*: Kraftwerk's visual counterpoint to their futuristic music was to present themselves as belonging to a bygone era. But the pronounced retro styling not only stressed the contrast with their revolutionary sound, it also served as a pointer to the nostalgic elements the album sought to evoke: German romanticism ('Franz Schubert'), the dream of a peaceful Europe in the early twentieth century, before it was ravaged by two world wars ('Europe Endless'), and the elegance and opulence of baroque architecture ('Hall of Mirrors').

Firm evidence of Kraftwerk's fascination with the technological aspects of the early twentieth century and the Nazi era can be seen in the video to the title song. For instance, sequences from a film commissioned by the Nazis were used. Called *Das*

Stahltier (*The Steel Animal*, 1935), the film veered strongly towards an Expressionist aesthetic and did not convey the celebratory message that the Nazis had hoped for, which is why it was banned.[38]

As well as documentary footage and scenes showcasing the band on board a train, the video also features several short sequences showing an odd-looking train, a *Schienenzeppelin* (rail zeppelin), an experimental railcar with a striking streamlined design featuring a rear propeller. Only one prototype, capable of accelerating to speeds of up to 200 km/ph, was built, in 1929, and it was dismantled in 1939. The futuristic design proved impractical for commercial use: its construction made it impossible to pull extra wagons.

In addition to the footage of the actual rail zeppelin, there are also stunning sequences showing a model of the city of the *Schienenzeppelin* speeding through a futuristic cityscape that strongly resembled the mega-architecture to be found in the pioneering sci-fi film *Metropolis* from 1927. The model was built from Styrofoam by Karl Kleefisch, the designer of the *Man-Machine* artwork, at the behest of Hütter and Schneider. What we see in these convincing trick sequences is a future that was never realized, or to put it another way, a future whose unfulfilled promises haunt the present. As such, it represents a prime example of the aesthetic strategy of retro-futurism that is deeply imprinted throughout Kraftwerk's œuvre.

But *Trans-Europe Express* is also very much an album about the present, and in particular the situation faced by Kraftwerk after the success of *Autobahn*. Touring America, their success in France following *Radio-Activity* and the British tour were significant experiences for the young musicians. This first-hand contact with other cultures (whose languages Hütter and Schneider spoke fluently) allowed Kraftwerk to come to a better idea of their own identity: 'Thanks to these transatlantic trips we discovered our cultural identity as Europeans. Distance allows us [. . .] to look at our own culture from a new perspective.'[39] Not that, as a German, Hütter needed a lesson in cultural awareness:

You travel for one hour [from Düsseldorf] then you come into a completely different country. We live a half an hour from Holland and Belgium. If you travel another hour, you get into France. So, it's a mix of different cultures on the Rhineland [. . .] My passport says I'm German but, in reality, the Rhine where we live has been German, has been Roman, French, has been Dutch, even Russian. The country has been taken over and over again by different cultures so we are really a cultural supermarket.[40]

From a German perspective, living in the heart of the European continent means more than the convenience of being able to travel quickly to interesting cities. It brings an awareness of European history, not just the long-term cultural perspective Ralf Hütter describes above but also in terms of a painful awareness of the genocidal operations that ravaged Europe in the forties. Germans such as Hütter and Schneider are very aware of the fact that there exists no 'innocent' landscape in Central and Eastern Europe: even though there may be no visible signs or reminders left, travelling across Europe means traversing the bloody battlefields of the Great War and the sites of murderous crimes – former concentration camps or torture prisons – of the Second World War.

There is a sense of place and history that differs greatly from the English approach, which could be said to present the past in a National Trust style of 'heritage'. Traditionally, in the UK, history has been treated as the succession of kings and queens, of happy and glorious events, of cultural icons like Shakespeare and great leaders like Churchill; it celebrates bravery and charming idiosyncrasy, covering over traces of the more unsavoury aspects of British history.

Hitler and the Holocaust are taught ad nauseam in schools, while students entering university may have never heard of Oswald Mosley and his British Union of Fascists. Equally, they may be ignorant of the fact that the term 'concentration camp' was coined by the British army for the facilities for imprisoning civilians under terrible conditions during the Boer War.

The German sense of history is very different. Germany has a terrible past, but it refuses to turn that past into history. This is one reason why Germans in particular, having belonged to a nation of perpetrators, support the vision of a peaceful Europe with open borders and free movement and a spirit of mutual cooperation towards an 'ever closer union'. Many Germans, too, have misgivings, perhaps justified, about the European Union, feeling it is an institution (mis)managed by ineffective bureaucrats who seem unable to deal with the great challenges of our time. But despite its many flaws, the EU zone with its free borders and common currency represents the palpable reality of the European project – the political goal of successfully ending chauvinistic nationalism and warfare on the continent.

It is against this background that *Trans-Europe*

Express has to be understood. The opening track, 'Europe Endless', sings the praises of a continent without borders. (It was originally intended to serve as the album title.) In retrospect, the epic track can be described as prophetic, given that eight years after its release the abolition of internal border controls within the European Union was achieved with the Schengen Agreement of 1985.[41] It runs just short of ten minutes and is based on a melodic structure somewhat reminiscent of 'Autobahn'. With its elegant electronic choirs and forward-pushing rhythm, the music creates the image of a never-ending journey across a beautiful continent, as expressed in the endlessly repeated, trance-inducing mantra 'Europe endless'.

This idealized journey is structured through the various sights that would meet the eye of a train passenger looking out of a carriage window. The train ride creates a continent in which the various regions and nations seem to have merged into one long row of nostalgic impressions:

Parks, hotels and palaces
Europe endless
Promenades and avenues
Europe endless
Real life and postcard views
Europe endless

Set against the gritty urban realism the punk music of the time was espousing, 'Europe Endless' paints a romantic albeit melancholic picture of the continent grounded in the natural beauty of its landscape. Hütter remarked of the track: 'We travelled all over Europe, and [. . .] realized that Europe is mostly parks and old hotels. . . "promenades and avenues". . . real life, but in a world of postcards.'[42]

This last point is important and is made explicit in the lyrics: the 'and' between 'real life' and 'postcard views' is a disjunctive one. Kraftwerk know full well that there is a difference between reality on the one hand and the idealized perception of a European past on the other.

Though the vision conjured up by the track aims to evoke the utopian goal of an endless Europe, its nostalgic references to palaces and promenades point back in time to an image of an idealized, cosmopolitan Europe of the early twentieth century. Of course, later, Europe became caught up in the maelstrom of nationalistic hatred and racial aggression: the song 'is a utopian hymn to a Europe without borders that has its source in another of Kraftwerk's apparent daydreams; a 20th century without the scar of Nazi Germany scored into the heart of Europe'.[43] The song has a split perspective: it is looking back and forward at the same time, a dual approach that mirrors the distinct contrast between the nostalgic photo of the band on the album sleeve and the futuristic music on the record.

Though it is not made explicit in 'Europe Endless', as it is the opening track on an album called *Trans-Europe Express* listeners would naturally assume that the seemingly endless journey through a Europe devoid of national borders would be a ride on one of the Trans Europ Express (TEE) luxury trains indicated by the title. The transnational TEE network was in operation from the late fifties up until the early nineties. At the height of its success in the mid-seventies, it connected 130 cities across Western Europe with regular high-speed services every two hours. The TEE system represented a modern, if expensive, lifestyle: only first-class travel was offered. Kraftwerk, as might be expected, regularly took this opportunity to travel across Europe.

From the *Autobahn* to the railway, from the car to the train: this is the trajectory of Kraftwerk's engagement with means of transportation. But why? There are four answers to this question. Firstly, the Kling Klang studio was only a short walk away from the main station in Düsseldorf, so the nearest TEE stop was literally round the corner. Leaving their studio, band members could see the trains on the main line running to and from the station. Secondly, making an album about Europe and travelling on the TEE was an obvious choice to follow *Autobahn*, which was about car travel across Germany.

Thirdly, the railway, like the car industry and the *Autobahn* network, can be seen historically as a key German application of technology: the first railway line in Germany was opened in 1835 to connect the Bavarian cities of Fürth and Nuremberg. In 1885, Germany's railway network was the largest in Europe, running to a total length of approximately 40,000 kilometres (far outstripping the closest contender, Great Britain, with a length of around 30,000 kilometres).

Fourthly, the railway was a forceful symbol of modernization because of its role as a driving force of industrialization. However, in the specific case of German history, it is (like the *Autobahn*) a strongly ambivalent symbol: the Nazis used the railway system to transport deportees to death camps. The Holocaust thus fused together barbaric mass murder and modern technology.

Sadly, the Germans were leaders in this respect, too. The apex of this atrocious development was the industrialized process of genocide in the camps, aptly described as 'death factories'. The *Reichsbahn*'s instrumental role in the murder of many hundreds of thousands of victims through deporting them in trans-European trains is remembered today by several memorials at train stations throughout Germany.

The French journalist Paul Alessandrini claims that he inspired the idea behind *Trans-Europe Express*: while dining with the band in Le Train Bleu, a magnificently stylish restaurant in the Gare de Lyon railway station in Paris, he told Hütter and Schneider: 'With the kind of music you do, which is kind of like an electronic blues, railway stations and trains are very important in your universe, you should do a song about the Trans Europ Express.'[44]

The image of a train also provided the perfect metaphor for Kraftwerk's aesthetic concept of technology and progress. Furthermore, it encapsulated the band's ethos of treating everyday objects as potential music-makers: if you pay attention to the noises made by your car, Hütter explained, 'you'll realize that it is a musical instrument'.[45] The same applies, perhaps even more so, to the train. *Trans-Europe Express* was, in a way, a repeat of the *Autobahn* formula but on a musically superior level.

With its tripartite structure and hypnotic beat, the 'Trans-Europe Express' suite is very sophisticated; it *transcribes* the noise of the wheels on the steel tracks into music (instead of merely translating the movement of car travel into a motorik beat).

'Movement interests us, instead of a static or motionless situation. All the dynamism of industrial life, of modern life.'[46] The band became a means to turn the sound of everyday forms of travel and transportation into electronic music which now, unlike 'Autobahn', on which there were acoustic instruments, used machines exclusively.

'Kraftwerk had perfected the synthesis of pop music and avant-garde sounds that has preoccupied them,'[47] commented Bussy. They had indeed realized the old dream of the Dadaist and Futurist movements of the early twentieth century to re-create industrial noise and everyday sounds with music. There are various examples of modernist efforts to turn the sound of train travel into music, the most noteworthy perhaps being Arthur Honegger's symphonic poem 'Pacific 231', composed in 1923 as a homage to the sound of the steam locomotive of the same name.

In Walter Ruttman's documentary film *Berlin: Die Sinfonie der Großstadt* (1927), trains feature heavily as indicators of the forward propulsion that is the hallmark of modernism. Cinema's particular interest in trains can be traced even further back, to the late nineteenth century: the fifty-second silent movie *Train Pulling into a Station* (1896) by the Lumière brothers is one of the very first cinematographic productions and a true avatar of modernism.

What Kraftwerk impressively created with 'Trans-Europe Express' was the evocation of a sense of speed and propulsion within the framework of pop music, and without resorting to the complicated arrangements that contemporary avant-garde composers require for the purpose. The track is one of their great achievements: a monotonous yet urgent electronic beat you can dance to which simultaneously sounds recognizably like a train.

As Hütter boasted, with justification: 'No other band could evoke the world of trains better than us, I think. The metallic music, metal on metal . . .'[48] Their danceable, futuristic music was eminently infectious, neither arty nor boring – and not just trans-Europe but also trans-Atlantic, as indicated by its chart success in the US.

The album also did very well in France, maintaining the momentum of *Radio-Activity*'s positive reception there. Kraftwerk's French record-company rep, Maxime Schmitt, did a sterling job of promoting Kraftwerk: a million copies of the 'Radioactivity' single were sold in France. In addition to the English-language version of *Trans-Europe Express*, there was also a French version containing 'Showroom Dummies' with French lyrics. The link to France, which paved the way for *Tour de France* a quarter of a century later, is established by the lyrics of 'Trans-Europe Express', which mark out the French capital as the starting point of the trans-European journey: 'Rendezvous on Champs-Élysées/Leave Paris in the morning on TEE/ Trans-Europe Express'.[49]

More than a mere nod to their French record-buyers, the journey from Paris to Düsseldorf alludes to the historical link between Germany and France. Since the French Revolution of 1789, Franco-German relations have been fraught, with wars, chauvinistic humiliation and acts of political revenge-taking. Given this *Erbfeindschaft* (hereditary enmity), which lasted until 1945, it seemed utterly inconceivable that France and Germany could turn into the driving forces of European integration in the immediate post-war period. Yet this is what happened.

Building on their personal friendship, the two political leaders Chancellor Konrad Adenauer and President Charles de Gaulle proactively drove forward greater political integration with the rest of Europe. Part and parcel of this political process was the cultural exchange between the countries, which aimed to foster a shared European cultural identity. Kraftwerk's track belongs firmly in this category: it celebrates the route between Paris and Düsseldorf, often travelled by the band members, a journey described by Hütter as 'spiritually European'.[50]

Acknowledging their most prominent fan from England, Kraftwerk sent their regards to David Bowie in the lyrics to 'Trans-Europe Express'. They did so not simply by name-checking him but also by clearly alluding to Bowie's 1976 album, *Station to Station*: 'From station to station back to Düsseldorf City/Meet Iggy Pop and David Bowie'. Bowie had played the A-side of *Radio-Activity* over the PA before his concerts on the Isolar tour to promote *Station to Station*. The sixty-four-date tour ran from February to May 1976, and Bowie's patronage helped to win Kraftwerk fans among a large international audience that may have not been familiar with the band. Bowie's Düsseldorf concert was particularly poignant, as the audience, by all accounts, was surprised to hear a local band.[51]

'With a ceaselessly mutable quicksilver shimmer, *Trans-Europe Express* is all at once antique, timeless, retro and contemporary. Its status as modern electronic music's birth certificate is well earned, but its hallowed reputation should never be allowed to disguise its true value and power as a work of art.'[52] Chris Power is right, but what makes the title track a work of art is that train wheels, as everybody knows, sound different from the beat of 'Trans-

Europe Express'. The amazing sense of thrust and velocity the music conjures up is down to the modulations that Schneider added to the rhythm programmed by Hütter, and the pattern for the drums played by Bartos.

Metallic Repercussions: In Germany and Beyond

Arguably, though, the central two minutes of *Trans-Europe Express* are the ferocious 'Metal on Metal'. Located in the middle of the 'Trans-Europe Express' suite, it is bookended by the title track and (in the German version) the outro 'Abzug'. Together, they form thirteen amazing minutes of electronic music, but the pounding anvil work of 'Metal on Metal' stands out. The origin of the track is unclear. Flür claims that the idea for it came from him,[53] while Bartos says that he himself was not at all involved in its recording.[54]

The track is supposed to simulate the noise of metal train wheels on a metal bridge. Kraftwerk tried all sorts of sound sources until they got it right: the clanging of metal pipes hitting each other, the noise made by applying a hammer to a bathtub or a washbowl, and so on. Apparently, the solution was to apply hammer blows to a wheelbarrow for the low frequencies and to a shelf made out of zinc to achieve the high pitch. In any case, the result sounds fantastic: Simon Reynolds described 'Metal on Metal' as 'a funky iron foundry that sounded like a Luigi Russolo Art of Noises megamix for a futurist discotheque'.[55]

David Stubbs reminds us that 'Trans-Europe Express' is 'one of a handful of the most influential tracks in the entire canon of popular music'.[56] The highly danceable combination of electronic pop music and avant-garde soundscapes resonated particularly with black communities in the US. Afrika Bambaataa, whose 'Planet Rock' would fuse African-American and German musical cultures in an exciting new way, said: 'I don't think they even knew how big they were among the black masses in '77 when they came out with *Trans-Europe Express*. When that came out I thought that was one of the weirdest records I ever heard in my life.'[57]

The metal machine sounds from North Rhine-Westphalia stimulated creative new ways of conceptualizing and recontextualizing music in a different cultural milieu. What had begun as an attempt by comfortably off middle-class Germans to make an album that expressed their 'cultural identity as Europeans'[58] provided underprivileged black communities of America with the sonic material to create music that in turn served as an expression of their cultural identity.

Once more, Hütter and Schneider would experience a moment of bafflement and delight upon suddenly hearing their own music in America. During a visit to a New York nightclub in the autumn of 1977, Hütter reported hearing 'Metal on Metal' on the PA when he arrived: 'So I thought, "Oh, they're playing the new album," but it went on for ten minutes and I thought, "What's happening? That track is only something like two or three minutes." Later, I went to ask the DJ and he had two copies of the record and was mixing the two.'[59]

Also worth a mention is the title track of Visage's second album, released in 1982. Called 'The Anvil', its pounding beat bears more than a passing resemblance to 'Metal on Metal'. But the same can be said about many British synth bands and musicians – just think of early Depeche Mode or Peter Gabriel's *Security*, with its furious drumming on tracks such as 'I Have the Touch' or 'Shock the Monkey'. It is of course no coincidence that Gabriel chose to release this album, as well as others, in a German-language version.

The leftist British collective Test Dept absorbed Kraftwerk's notion of *industrielle Volksmusik* and re-created it with their percussive sound, literally made by drumming metal on metal. The group, from London, initially played its visceral, highly politically charged music mostly on 'found' objects gathered from scrap yards. Often accompanied by film projections and slide shows, Test Dept's intensely energetic concerts were the opposite of Kraftwerk's cool, controlled performances, but the aesthetic links between the bands are easy to detect.

For example, rather than playing conventional concerts, Test Dept strive to deliver an overwhelming, large-scale audiovisual experience on stage. Like Kraftwerk, they aim to transform the noise of factories into the sounds of *industrielle Volksmusik*, and Test Dept's use of a collective, impersonal and somewhat dehumanized public image strongly resembles Kraftwerk's concept of the man-machine and their self-stylization as 'music workers'.

One fascinating aside is the strong reception Kraftwerk received in Slovenia, as evidenced by the two volumes of *Trans Slovenia Express* compilations. These appeared between 1994 and 2005 and contain nearly thirty Kraftwerk covers by Slovenian bands. The most interesting interpretations are by Laibach. Founded in 1980, in what was then communist Yugoslavia, the artist collective, based in Ljubljana, have created their own *Gesamtkunstwerk* over the course of the last thirty-five years as part of the NSK (*Neue*

Slowenische Kunst) movement. Their brilliant track 'Bruderschaft' ('Brotherhood'), which opens the second volume of *Trans Slovenia Express*, impressively adapts Kraftwerk's sound (with evident nods to 'Trans-Europe Express') and contains clever allusions to their lyrics. The four-minute track sounds as if it emerged straight out of the Kling Klang studio.

Laibach's guiding aesthetic of 'retrogarde' is partly derived from Kraftwerk's take on retrofuturism: both groups return artistically to the unredeemed potentials of earlier avant-garde movements in order to revitalize them for the present.[60] (Rammstein, in turn, copied and trivialized Laibach's highly ironic flirting with totalitarian imagery to forge their own, inferior, imitation.)

Kraftwerk's impact was also felt in their native land. *Trans-Europe Express* served as inspiration for industrial bands like Die Krupps, with their remarkable steel-bashing debut 'Stahlwerksynfonie' ('Steelworks symphony') of 1981. This blinding track lasts nearly a quarter of an hour and, in addition to metal on metal, features power drills over the standard set of guitars and drums. The band, which also hails from Düsseldorf, even built an instrument called the 'steelophone' which they could take on tour with them to re-create their frenzied percussion on stage.

Berlin's Einstürzende Neubauten took the title 'Metal on Metal' literally, too, using all sorts of metal items for percussion instead of traditional instruments. One of their earliest recordings is 'Stahlmusik' ('Steel Music'), and even though, initially, they went down a far more extremist path than Kraftwerk, there can be no doubt that the industrial sound from Düsseldorf was one of their influences. The same applies to DAF, or Deutsch-Amerikanische Freundschaft (German-American friendship), consisting of Gabi Delgado-López and Robert Görl, yet another Düsseldorf band, whose stripped-down electronic version of motorik music was clearly influenced by Kraftwerk.

Trans-Europe Express set a new standard in electronic pop music. In the words of Martyn Ware of The Human League and Heaven 17: '*Trans-Europe Express* had everything: it was retro yet futuristic, melancholic yet timeless, technical, modern and forward-looking yet also traditional. You name it, it had it all.'[61] When Alessandrini asked Hütter whether he thought people who wanted to know about Europe in 1976 would only have to listen to Kraftwerk, he responded with: 'Yes, I hope so.'[62]

4. 'WE ARE THE ROBOTS': FROM *THE MAN-MACHINE* TO *COMPUTER WORLD*

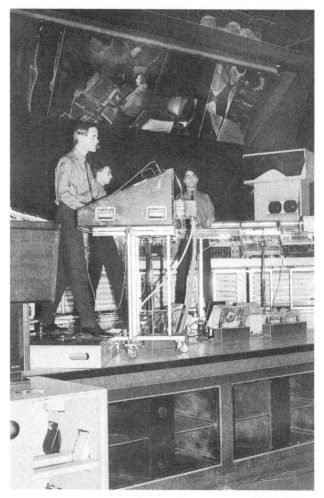

Concert in Oyten (North Germany), 14 December
1981, during the *Computer World* tour.

'The Man-Machine is our acoustic concept, and Kraftwerk means power plant – if you plug in the electricity, then it starts to work. It's feedback.'

– Florian Schneider

The Man-Machine: Kraftwerk's Central Concept Album

Standing in front of a closed curtain, waiting for the concert to begin – then, the moment that never fails to send a shiver down my spine. And I assume other Kraftwerk fans feel no different. It has become an established ritual at Kraftwerk's concerts since the mid-seventies that a disembodied, synthesized voice announces the band, like a robot compère: '*Meine Damen und Herren, heute Abend, aus Deutschland, Kraftwerk, die Mensch-Maschine*' (Ladies and Gentlemen, tonight, from Germany, Kraftwerk, the man-machine).

Kraftwerk are the man-machine. The notion of connecting, perhaps even hybridizing, the human and the technological represents the central artistic tenet of their œuvre from *Autobahn* onwards. By the time of their 1975 US tour, newspaper ads were already announcing, in German, Kraftwerk as 'Mensch-Maschine'. In an interview published in the same year, Florian Schneider is on record saying: 'Kraftwerk is not a band. It is a concept. We call it *die Mensch-Maschine*. We are not the band [. . .] Kraftwerk is the vehicle for our ideas.'[1] But it wasn't until three albums down the line, in May 1978, that the band released *The Man-Machine*.

The Man-Machine stands out in Kraftwerk's formidable body of work not just because it contains their only chart-topping song, the UK number one 'The Model': more significantly, it represents Kraftwerk's artistic centrepiece, as it embodies the 'corporate identity' of the band, both conceptually and visually. The black-and-red colour scheme (with a pinch of white) has dominated the band's iconography ever since; the band's website, for example, uses the same minimalist colour scheme, as do many of the posters which have advertised their concerts since 2011.

On the original album artwork, the band members appear as uniform would-be robots, dressed in grey trousers, red shirts and black ties, their pale faces supplying a splash of white to complement the colour composition. (Their heads, in turn, can be seen as a recurrence of the colour scheme in miniature: white skin and black hair are supplemented with bright red lips, which give the band members a curiously camp look.)

The Album

With *Trans-Europe Express*, Kraftwerk created a deliberate discord between the nostalgia-evoking retro visuals and the notion of music that was ahead of its time. *The Man-Machine*, on the other hand, featured strikingly futuristic styling, chiming with the music, which sounds technically perfect yet never sterile. The aspirations and expectations that *Trans-Europe Express* fostered were fully honoured by its successor. As Bussy claims, the album was 'stunningly ahead of its time'.[2]

But there were also critical voices, among them Stubbs, who pointed out that 'on certain tracks [. . .] they were playing catch-up with the innovations by Giorgio Moroder and Robbie Wedel',[3] who had enjoyed immense success with the disco hit 'I Feel Love'. Such reservations, however, justified though they may be, remain the exception. More representative of the received opinion on *The Man-Machine* is Martyn Ware (Human League / Heaven 17), who appreciated its artistic success as a *Gesamtkunstwerk*: The album 'was stone-cold urban and design-led. [. . .] To me this was the soundtrack of the cities.

It was like a manifesto that wrapped up graphic design, photography and music, all in the same bag.'[4]

A true Kraftwerk evergreen is the romantic 'Neon Lights', with its lilting melody. The song is a reflection of Düsseldorf at night, paying tribute to the many colourful neon signs that advertise shops, hotels and bars in the band's hometown. 'Neon Lights' is a frequently underrated classic in the Kraftwerk œuvre, a sublimely atmospheric piece. Andy Gill in his review of *The Man-Machine* for the *NME* perceptively hailed the album, stating that its artistic 'success is rooted in the conceptual framework Kraftwerk impose on their work', but he did not single out either the title track or 'The Robots'.

Instead, without hesitation, he names 'Neon Lights' the 'best track on the album'.[5] Indeed, the captivating melody has been described as 'a sonic refutation of the allegations that Kraftwerk had no soul'.[6] The esteem in which the song is held by fellow musicians can be gauged by the dozens of cover versions that have been made: U2, Simple Minds (who also named their 2001 covers album after the song) and OMD are the most prominent acts to pay homage to it, but it is probably Luna's version that best catches the romantic mood of this beguiling piece of music and translates it into guitar music.

'The Model', too, is about Düsseldorf, the

fashion capital of Germany at the time. Featuring the only female protagonist in their discography, it is also the band's most straightforward pop song. Though it might seem sacrilegious to some fans, there are some who would argue that 'The Model', despite being Kraftwerk's first and only number-one hit single,[7] hardly ranks among Kraftwerk's best work musically. There are no exciting electronic sound effects on this track, the melody is rather bland and becomes boring after a few listens. What's more, it doesn't quite fit on *The Man-Machine*: the lyrical themes of commerce, sex, drinking and dancing at a chic nightclub are at odds with the decidedly futuristic orientation of the album.[8]

There are two instrumentals on *The Man-Machine*: 'Spacelab' and 'Metropolis'. The former alludes to a project by the German rocket scientist Wernher von Braun, who was reputedly namechecked by Kraftwerk in interviews. Braun worked for both the Nazis and NASA and proposed the utopian idea of setting up a permanent space station orbiting Earth as a basis for experiments.[9] The title of the latter track refers to the great Expressionist film of the same name. This reference deserves a closer look, as it is vital for the aesthetics of Kraftwerk, as Hütter explained: 'Our roots were in the culture that was stopped by Hitler; the school of Bauhaus and German Expressionism.'[10]

German Expressionism not only extended to the fine arts but proved pioneering in cinema. Great visionary directors such as Fritz Murnau (*Nosferatu*, 1922), Robert Wiene (*Das Cabinet des Dr Caligari*, 1919) and Fritz Lang (*Metropolis*, 1927) were groundbreaking in their art, establishing entire genres such as the vampire or science-fiction film. It was the latter in particular who was of interest to Kraftwerk. Hütter and Schneider, as Bartos presumes, must have long been familiar with Lang's masterpiece, as private screenings were held in the home of the Schneider family.

To refresh their memory, they took Bartos along to a public screening of *Metropolis* when they were working on *The Man-Machine*. The screening was so crowded the musicians had to watch it standing in the back of the cinema. The fact that the evil scientist Rotwang adresses the robot he created as *Maschinenmensch* ('machine-person', or 'machine-man') may well have inspired Hütter and Schneider to twist around the two components of the word to arrive at the German album title: *Mensch-Maschine*.[11]

Questioned shortly after the release of *The Man-Machine* in 1978, Ralf Hütter admitted:

> We were very much influenced by the futuristic silent films of Fritz Lang [. . .] We feel that we are the sons of that type of science fiction

cinema. We are the band of *Metropolis*. Back in the 1920s, people were thinking technologically about the future in physics, film, radio, chemistry, mass transport . . . everything but music. We feel that our music is a continuation of this early futurism. [. . .] Historically, we feel that if there were a music group in *Metropolis*, maybe Kraftwerk would have been that band.[12]

Kraftwerk would have been the perfect band to produce a new soundtrack to *Metropolis*.[13] (Allegedly, they were once asked but turned the offer down.) The six-minute instrumental on *The Man-Machine* gives an indication of what that soundtrack might have sounded like.[14]

Lang's *Metropolis* was a major source of inspiration in terms of retro-futurist imaginings of what future cities would look like. The seemingly contradictory concept of retro-futurism fuses the futuristic with the nostalgic to create a haunted sense of a temporal 'in-between'. Time is out of joint, which allows for surprising insights. Manifestations of retro-futurism can be found in the worlds of architecture, design, music, literature, film and video games. The phenomenon can take many shapes and forms; it is a pluralistic movement and cannot be reduced to a normative aesthetic.

Kraftwerk were fascinated by it. As Hütter stated, Kraftwerk had the desire to 'look forwards as well as backwards at the same time, the French call it retro-futurism'.[15] One of retro-futurism's main strategies is the creation of tension by depicting past imaginings of the future that have subsequently proved obsolete – such as the previously mentioned high-speed train fitted with a giant propeller that can be seen in the video for 'Trans-Europe Express'. Hütter explained the retro-futurist thrust of Kraftwerk thus: 'What we were much considering was the simultaneity of past, present and future today. I think visions and memories synchronise together, and I think certain things from a little way back look more towards the future than things that are pseudo-modern today.'[16]

Man-Machines: The Cultural-historical Background

Another important theme in the Kraftwerk aesthetic cosmos also derived from *Metropolis* – the image of the robot. For the album launch parties held in Paris and New York, Kraftwerk had look-alike dummies of the four band members wearing the red shirt/black tie made by the famous designer of shop-window mannequins Heinrich Obermaier.

The assembled journalists were asked to interview the dummies instead of the band members themselves.

The German premiere of the mannequins was on 1 April 1978 on the TV programme *Rock Pop* for a performance of 'The Robots'. To welcome the band, the presenter shook the hand of the dummy representing Hütter. The TV appearance was pretty impressive: the camera alternately showed the dummies behind the equipment and the members of the band playing it. In one sequence, the band can be seen dancing robotically to the music. There are frequent close-ups of the mannequins' faces and at one point the lips of Hütter singing the chorus are superimposed on those of his dummy double, creating the scary impression that it has come alive.

At the time, there wasn't a band on the planet who were pulling off stunts like this. Imposters, plagiarists and satirists have since found it very easy to imitate the iconic cover image. Devoted fans, too, have adopted the look. One American couple got married in the Kraftwerk uniform. At concerts, some audience members will be dressed like this, while the band sometimes picks 'Man-Machine' to begin their set as a statement of intent.

For many years now, 'The Robots', the other song from *The Man-Machine* that could be said to encapsulate their ethos, has been the first encore of most Kraftwerk shows. When the curtain is raised, the audience sees the four mechanical dummies representing, or rather, substituting for the band. Already in their third generation, these dummies 'perform' their theme tune to the delight of the audience, lending a striking validation to the proud assertion: 'We are the robots.'

Robots, as mechanical *doppelgängers* of the band, and the conceptual notion of the man-machine are of course closely linked. They occupy a fundamental position in the artistic self-representation of Kraftwerk. For this reason, it is both necessary and fascinating to look at the cultural-historical background of *The Man-Machine*. Only then can we fully understand the tradition against which the band operates in adopting an identity based on transhuman imagery. Clearly, the notion of the robot is deeply futuristic, as it epitomizes the potential moment of evolution at which man and technology would merge.

But *The Man-Machine* also points to the past, giving the album a cultural-historic depth and emphasizing the perception that the idea is only a transitory stage between past and future. The cover artwork is strongly typographic and features the album title in four languages. The French translation, *L'Homme machine*, is a nod to the infamous tract by the philosopher Julien Offray de La Mettrie. *L'Homme machine*, in which La Mettrie proposed the radically atheist view of a materialistic unity between body and soul, caused a considerable scandal when it appeared in 1747.

His heretical pamphlet attacked one of the foundations of the unholy alliance of Church, state and society: it questioned the metaphysical notion that the soul was separate from the body and therefore subject to the power of theology. The *enfant terrible* of French materialism instead advocated a monistic model of interdependence between the body and the soul. Drawing on and extending an existing school of philosophy which claimed that the human body functioned according to the rules of mechanics and hydraulics, La Mettrie polemically argued that the *entire* human being (that is, body and soul together) constituted a machine.

This was a bold claim at the time, radicalizing previous advances in knowledge by Sir Francis Bacon in the natural sciences and by Galileo in terms of a mechanical understanding of nature. The accursed philosopher La Mettrie, whose books were burned and who had to seek refuge at the liberal court of Frederick the Great in Berlin, eventually came to be considered far ahead of his time, an accolade that may of course also be attached to Kraftwerk's run of great albums during the second half of the seventies.

Two points are of particular relevance here. Firstly, despite his radicalism in attacking the traditional notion of the divine freedom of man, La Mettrie never questioned the existence of the human soul. The same applies to Kraftwerk, according to Maxime Schmitt (their French record rep): 'For me Kraftwerk has a soul, even though it was electronic and mathematic.'[17] Ralf Hütter, too, claims that their machines do have a soul: 'The dynamism of the machines, the "soul" of the machines, has always been a part of our music,' he declared, adding, 'Trance belongs to repetition, and everybody is looking for trance in life [. . .] So, the machines produce an absolutely perfect trance.'[18]

La Mettrie's philosophical equation of man with machinery immediately suggested an attempt to reverse this dichotomy between body and soul. Coincidentally, it was in the eighteenth century that the first mechanical automatons appeared. These creations complemented, even if they did not demonstrate, the validity of the man-machine concept by literally making the metaphor. It is not without relevance here that many of these early automatons were built to impersonate musicians.

Take, for example, the flute player created by Jacques de Vaucanson in 1738. Bellows hidden inside and operated by clockwork created an airflow that was channelled to the instrument at the mouth of the machine. Similarly, brothers Pierre and Henri-Louis Jaquet-Droz built an organ-player automaton in the early 1770s which was able to play five different melodies on a real instrument. The mechanical head of the organ player could follow the movements of the mechanical hands, and its eyes looked at the audience at regular intervals.

The French predilection for musical robots continued well into the twentieth century. Kraftwerk imitators Daft Punk with their robot image are an obvious point of reference, but more pertinent and interesting here are Les Robots Music, an animatronic orchestra built in the fifties. They were a mechanical trio – drummer, accordion player and saxophonist, all playing on real instruments – made of sheet metal, musical robots that looked as if they had jumped out of a children's TV programme from the seventies. A popular funfair attraction up until the sixties, Les Robots Music also released several successful albums comprising cover versions of French and international pop hits, as well as political songs.

The Iconic Cover

The implicit link between the man-machine concept and the communist connotations of the album artwork did not escape the West German record-buying public when *The Man-Machine* was released. However, perceptive Germans would inevitably also be reminded of the colour scheme of the Nazi flag: a red background with a white circle containing the swastika symbol in black. Taking the paramilitary look into account as well, the imagery could not avoid evoking unwelcome associations at first glance, and the band must have been aware of this.

These flirtations with Nazi symbolism were dangerous. The associations of the colour code of the flag and the uniforms with the Nazi era also served as a reminder that the crimes of the past were possible only because far too many Germans had been – in the words of scholar Daniel Goldhagen – Hitler's 'willing executioners': like robots without conscience or moral compass, they had followed the orders of the Nazis. Deliberately intentional, Kraftwerk's aim in toying with fascist imagery was 'a way of getting an unwilling Germany to meet its past and to look itself in the mirror'.[19]

Yet the clearly dominant colour red conjures up the opposite political affiliation, particularly once the manifest visual allusions are recognized. The cover image was a homage to the work of the graphic designer El Lissitzky. He was an avant-garde artist and architect who worked in Germany as a cultural ambassador of the Soviet Union in the early twenties and had connections with the Bauhaus.

More of a duplication than a homage, as Hagström points out, is the artwork on the back of the album; it shows an excerpt from a graphic design published by El Lissitzky in a 1922 children's book called *Two Squares: A Suprematist Tale of Two Squares in Six Constructions*. The importance given to typography is also derived from this revolutionary communist artist. For those who lack knowledge of modernist graphic design, a note on the back cover spelled it out: 'Artwork Karl Klefisch/Inspired by El Lissitzky'.

There were also nods to communism with the Russian translation of the album title on the cover and the fact that the band is looking eastwards. This was a pretty brave statement in 1978. The tensions of the Cold War remained, and there was public hysteria at the left-wing terrorism of the Red Army Faction (also known as the Baader-Meinhof Group) in Germany. After an attempt to hijack a Lufthansa plane failed disastrously at Mogadishu airport in October 1977, Andreas Baader and his fellow terrorists in Stammheim prison committed suicide. Baader, it turned out, had been able to hide a pistol inside his record player, despite regular searches of his prison cell, and how the terrorists managed to smuggle weapons into their supposedly high-security prison cells and take their lives in a concerted action was never fully explained. There were accusations of state murder, or at least tacit involvement. For several weeks, during the so-called 'German Autumn', the Federal Republic teetered on the brink of the gravest state crisis since its inception.

However, the political references in the *Man-Machine* artwork are not necessarily intended to be read as a reflection of Kraftwerk's politics. Coming roughly a decade after Hütter and Schneider's generation took to the streets in 1968, the cover image was strikingly futuristic yet it also had to be understood as an art-historical pointer to the radical era of constructivism – a time when revolutionary politics and revolutionary art were closely intertwined. *The Man-Machine* seems to express the hope that this fruitful link could be rekindled and revitalized in order to inaugurate a new era of German cultural self-confidence through the production of a revolutionary type of music.

The Robots are Taking Over

Socio-economic factors should also be considered a crucial backdrop to *The Man-Machine*: the rise of Krautrock in the late sixties coincided with the introduction of industrial robots in manufacturing in Europe. This particularly applied to car manufacturing, the backbone of the German economy. The German public's perception of the results of this progressive 'robotization' was made up of two contradictory strands. On the one hand, there was the frightening prospect of redundancy for those who (like my father) worked in branches of manufacturing that were increasingly embracing the new technology. TV reports showing Japanese car-production lines devoid of any human beings were seen with great unease as the future of German manufacturing. On the other, to my great delight as a child, robots invaded family life across the country and were busy conquering nurseries in the form of toys. *The Man-Machine* arrived just as expensive, hand-made, metal robot models were being increasingly replaced by mass-produced plastic models from the Far East. Robots became ubiquitous on TV and movie screens. As well as the endearing R2-D2 and C-3PO from the *Star Wars* (1977) universe, one puppetry TV series produced in the WDR studios in Cologne deserves a special mention: *Robbi, Tobbi und das Fliewatüüt* was pretty revolutionary TV at the time, blending puppets with real-life backgrounds. The four-part series remains popular today, a true classic of German children's TV.

A noticeable generational gap and an overall ambivalence in the attitude of Germans towards robotization existed during the late seventies. Kraftwerk's *Man-Machine* addressed and reflected this situation, as the album invited the listener to perceive technological advances as more of an opportunity than a threat. Certainly for children, robots, more than any other technological object in the Kraftwerk cosmos, exerted an obvious attraction and fascination, one that lasts to the present day. Just check out the many videos available on the Web showing school projects or father/son duos creatively engaging with the 'Robots' song.

What Exactly are 'The Robots'?

In a way, the 'generational conflict' of the seventies mirrored the cultural-historical ambivalence that has shaped our attitude towards men-machines, veering between menace and fascination. Ambivalence, too, emerges if one takes a closer look at the role of robots in the Kraftwerk world. Statements made by Hütter and Schneider on the subject are legion, yet fail to provide any clarity, as they are either inconclusive or contradictory, or both.

Once more, Kraftwerk placed the onus of interpreting their work in the hands of the listeners. Florian Schneider explained: 'The image of the robot is very important to us, it's stimulating to people's imaginations [. . .] The robots may be an image, a projection, a reflection, a mirror of what happens – I think people understand that. You don't have to explain it, I think the things speak for themselves.'[20]

When trying to understand a song, the first port of call is of course the lyrics. Frustratingly, in Kraftwerk's case, these are often too minimal to allow a definitive interpretation. All we know about the Kraftwerk robots is that, true to their purpose, they want to serve us: 'We are programmed just to do/Anything you want us to'. Furthermore, they run on rechargeable batteries and have a preference for dancing 'mekanik' – which supposedly is a dance style that suits a motorik beat.

Therefore, they are closely related to the showroom dummies on *Trans-Europe Express*: frustrated with their passive role, the dummies break through the glass of a window to go out dancing in a club in town – as impressively, though ironically, demonstrated by the four band members in the video to 'Showroom Dummies'.

The robots' proclaimed fondness for dancing, however, is at odds with the fact that the dressed-up mannequins presented at the launch of *The Man-Machine* were, obviously, unable to move. That ability was gained only by the robot doubles the band developed for the release of *The Mix* in 1991. Though fitted with mechanical arms and a torso, they had only metal tubes for legs. The current robot generation appears on stage wearing grey trousers to cover their obviously non-functional legs. Thanks to a moveable disc and small wheels, they do sway a little to the left and right while performing their theme song. But one can hardly describe this as dancing.

This forces us to state the obvious: even in their latest incarnation, the 'robots' are no more than fairly simple mechanical dummies and certainly not robots in the sense of a functional, mobile and artificially intelligent man-machine, as characterized in this definition: 'The term "robot" refers first of all to an automatic system capable of replacing people in the execution of complex tasks, founded on a sensory and kinetic interaction with the environment.'[21]

But that is the crucial point: to pretend that the dummies are robots – when everyone can plainly see they are not. Every time the curtain opens for the encore, the audience is facing a 'characteristically Kraftwerkian moment; what seems like an expression of faith in the cyborgian future is presented, if not satirically, then at least ironically – offered up, and undercut, simultaneously' because the stage robots 'seem to hark back to a mechanical past' rather than 'to the forthcoming convergence of man and machine'.[22]

It is therefore easy to criticize the robot dummies. In 1992, Karl Bartos said: 'In the beginning, I kind of liked the idea of the robots, because it was new, it was a good idea. But if you do the same thing ten years later it is ridiculous.'[23] He may be right, but he misses an important point: the discrepancy indicates that there is a distinction to be made between the playful and highly ironic exhibition of the mannequins-parading-as-robots and the conceptual notion of the Kraftwerk persona – that is to say, their artistic self-presentation as 'robots' – as a concrete manifestation of the man-machine concept. After all, it is not the mechanized dummies but the abstract Kraftwerk persona that claims: 'We are the robots!' Even though they are the very opposite of rock, Kraftwerk also like to work with an image they want to project.

However, their image is clearly recognizable as being based on an artistic concept. Of course, none of their fans thinks that Ralf Hütter and the other three Kraftwerkers are really robots or man-machines. This approach separates Kraftwerk from multimillionaires such as Bruce Springsteen or Bob Dylan, who play the role of lonesome songsmith and regular American guy.

With Kraftwerk, the robot business makes sense only if it is understood as the representation of an idea that Ralf Hütter and Florian Schneider must have found fascinating from the mid-seventies: the ambition to make future music, which required a complex interaction with the machines in their studio. As Schneider explained, these were neither master nor servant: 'It's rather a more sophisticated relationship. There is an interaction. Interaction on both sides.'[24]

What Exactly is a 'Man-Machine'?

Even though the title track of *The Man-Machine* unmistakeably constitutes the central paradigm of Kraftwerk's artistic concept, we come to know very little about this strange creature. The lyrics are even more minimal than those of 'The Robots'. And there are subtle differences between the German and English versions. According to the German lyrics, the man-machine is 'halb Wesen und halb Ding' (half a living being and half a thing). This creates a tension between two incongruous, antagonistic parts. In the

English version of the song, the anomalous creature is rendered as the more compact 'semi-human being', which reduces the crucial internal contradiction captured in the German version.

Ralf Hütter described the group's relationship to the electronic instruments of their trade as follows: 'We are playing the machines, the machines play us, it is really the exchange and the friendship we have with the musical machines which make us build a new music.'[25] Such a statement needs to be understood against the background of Kraftwerk's aim to define a unique identity, differentiating them not just from their Krautrock brethren but also, more importantly, from rock music as a semi-conservative genre.

In a joking reference to the lute played by German minstrels, Hütter remarked: 'The guitar is an instrument from medieval times. This entire business of rock music strikes us as entirely archaic. The music of a technicized world can only be made on instruments that have been devised by a technicized world.'[26] Kraftwerk comprehensively translated this conceptual idea into a new type of music. Their 'robo pop' (Hütter) or 'android doo-wop' (Simon Reynolds) was 'a conscious, deliberately constructed aesthetic offence to traditional rock values [. . .] where a sense of unbuttoned maleness, of hair and heart and emotive authenticity was paramount'.[27]

Hütter and Schneider certainly did not subscribe to the male stereotypes largely governing rock music. Alluding to the cliché that sees some rock guitarists treating their instrument on stage as if it were an extension of their sexual organ, Florian Schneider used the opportunity to pull the leg of an interviewer who questioned him when *The Man-Machine* was released: 'We love our machines,' he said, and added, 'We have an erotic relationship with them.'[28]

While there are a good number of female Kraftwerk fans, male enthusiasts certainly dominate at concerts. Criticism of Kraftwerk often focuses on the perceived sexism of their music, which evokes a male-dominated world almost devoid of female representation. And indeed, as soon as women do enter the Kraftwerk cosmos, as in the case of 'The Model', they are objectified through the male gaze, or are typecast as sex-driven beings who force the male singer to caution them about their compulsive behaviour: 'I don't want to be your sex object/Show some feeling and respect/I don't want to be your sex object/I've had enough and that's a fact'.

Surely 'Sex Object' has to be the oddest track in the Kraftwerk catalogue. Unlike the more modest 'Computer Love', it opts for a funkier treatment of the topic, featuring the closest Kraftwerk ever get to Giorgio Moroder's global smash hit 'I Feel Love', performed by Donna Summer. It fails to match the mechanistic repetition, icy electronics and motorik propulsion of Moroder's production; instead, it is more of a robo-pop version of an encounter between a (German-singing) male and a (Spanish-singing) female. In any case, it offers an interesting variation on the standard love song in reversing the role allocation between predatory male and passive female.

A number of all-female groups openly mimic Kraftwerk's visual identity. Take the British acts Ladytron or Client. Client is made up of the duo Sarah Blackwood and Katie Holmes (augmented by further female band members for their live incarnation). Playing synth-pop and electroclash that is reminiscent of the Kraftwerk sound, they appear onstage wearing clothes that give a clear nod to the man-machine aesthetic (although, typically, they wear the uniform of an airline hostess or shiny fetish outfits). With song titles such as 'Köln' or 'Leipzig', they reference Germany to underline their allegiances to Kraftwerk.

Also worth a mention are Craftwife, a Japanese trio best described as a Kraftwerk cosplay tribute band. They play generative, real-time music created by apps designed by their chief member, sound designer Takeko Akamatsu.[29] Appearing in an outfit copied straight from the *Man-Machine* look,

Craftwife present the striking image of a transnational 'woman-machine'.

The Man-Machine on Pedals

Some twenty-five years after *The Man-Machine* came out, Kraftwerk surprised their fans by releasing a new studio album. *Tour de France Soundtracks* (2003) celebrated cycling with a very Kraftwerkian twist: forward-thrusting music aims to mimic how man and bicycle fuse through the intense physical labour of pedalling over long distances. But more on that album later.

'Cycling is the man-machine, it's about dynamics, always continuing straight ahead, forwards, no stopping,'[30] enthused Hütter. 'The bicycle is already a musical instrument on its own. The noise of the bicycle chain and pedal and gear mechanism, for example, the breathing of the cyclist, we have incorporated all this in the Kraftwerk sound, injecting the natural sounds into the computers in the studio.'[31]

The rhythmic heavy breathing at the beginning of the eponymous 1983 single 'Tour de France' – apparently, Hütter ran up and down the stairs in the Kling Klang studio to record the sound – is the sonic equivalent of the simulated train noises on 'Trans-Europe Express'. Both sound sources perform a similar role in providing the rhythm. But Kraftwerk place a particular stress on breathing as a basic bodily function that signifies aliveness and bears a structural similarity to music. Kraftwerk's second album from 1972 featured an instrumental called 'Atem' ('Breath'), indicating the importance the sound of breathing has always played in their work: it is the sign of life in the man-machine.

'The Bauhaus in Electronic Sounds': Kraftwerk and Modernity

'Bauhaus' is not an unfamiliar term in British popular culture, thanks to the seminal Northampton Goth band of the same name, but it was also the groundbreaking school of architecture, design and fine arts founded in Weimar in 1919 and closed down by the Nazis in 1933. Its ambitious goal was to rethink design from the bottom up. The Bauhaus rejected traditional ideas, seeking to create a modern design fit for the newly formed democratic Germany.

As a reform movement, its vision was to change society through the introduction of a new, functionalist way of living. The distinction between form and function was to be erased while arts and crafts were merged to create a total work of art. It is hardly a coincidence that the Bauhaus was founded by an architect, Walter Gropius: bringing together areas as diverse as art, interior design, industrial design, graphic design and typography needed someone with the experience to oversee the implementation of grand projects.

Likewise, the student of architecture and the son of a renowned architect who were running the Kraftwerk project aimed to fuse music and image, man and machine, and to oversee the gradual development of their very own *Gesamtkunstwerk*: a total work of art unique to pop music involving the fusion of cover artwork, the design of box sets, video and photography, the use of typography, stage design and stage outfits, among other things. The influence of the Bauhaus cannot be overestimated; Kraftwerk were attempting nothing less than an update of the modernist project that was violently cut short by the Nazis.

The cover of *The Man-Machine* provides a pertinent example: a visual reference to the Bauhaus style. Based on a picture taken by the photographer and cameraman Günter Fröhling, it shows the band members positioned on a functionalist staircase. The image has echoes of one of the iconic paintings associated with the Bauhaus, Oskar Schlemmer's *Bauhaustreppe* (*Bauhaus Staircase*) from 1932, which depicts people on the staircase of the Bauhaus building in Dessau near Berlin. The constructivist design of the entire album artwork was another nod to the Bauhaus.

Typography played a special role in the Bauhaus cosmos, providing a modern visual form to convey their modernist ideas via their many publications. Kraftwerk understood the importance of typography in their *Gesamtkunstwerk* for the same reason, but also to create a visual coherence across their work. *Trans-Europe Express* is the first Kraftwerk album that demonstrates the importance of typography: the use of the Futura (!) typeface coupled with three horizontal lines is not just reminiscent of typographic designs of the twenties and thirties but also relates to railway tracks and conveys a sense of speed and movement.[32]

The Bauhaus belief that art should meet the needs of the new democratic society – a demand that in turn harks back to William Morris – found expression in the aspiration of Kraftwerk's *industrielle Volksmusik* to reflect the social and economic reality of industrialized West Germany in the postwar era. The Bauhaus certainly saw its project as a contribution to the social and political struggle of their generation to reform the Federal Republic by providing a new form of musical expression of an untainted, modern and positive German identity.

Hütter and Schneider, too, sought to develop aesthetic equivalents in response to the new post-war era in German (cultural) history. According to Stubbs: 'The iron and glass tubes, the symmetry and the right angles of Bauhaus design are like a visual transcription of the Kraftwerk sound – spotless, minimal, metal surfaces, to replace the ancient, baroque follies of the discredited old world, with all its errors and unfitness for purpose.'[33]

Modernism, the very keystone of Bauhaus principles, demanded rationality in approach, functionality in design and radically simplified forms devoid of ornamentation. These guidelines were applied by Gropius in his architectural work but also by Kraftwerk in their approach to making music with machines. What could be more quintessentially modern than a new kind of pop music that retires drummers and replaces them with drum machines and sequencers? Certainly 'few artists have so consistently conceived of their own artistic logic in terms of its immanent engagement with the latest means of musical production.'[34]

Also in accordance with the modernist notion of music is Kraftwerk's artistic self-designation, which rejects conventional musicianship and strives for technical definitions, such as 'music worker' or 'sound researcher': 'Our daily schedule of work lasts some eight to ten hours in the studio. We don't regard ourselves just as musicians but as *Musik-arbeiter* [music workers].'[35] Fittingly, the Kling Klang studio was described as a kind of experimental 'laboratory'. Hütter explained: 'We aim to create a total sound, not to make music in the traditional sense with complex harmony. A minimalistic approach is more important for us. We spend a month on the sound and five minutes on the chord changes.'[36]

'Numbers' from the album *Computer World* may be cited as the prime example of Kraftwerk's approach of fusing minimalism with functionality in electronic music. The track represents a radical exercise in reduction. An almost brutal piece of music with its relentless drum pattern, it is impossible for a human percussionist to play. This mesmerizing track emerged out of the daily experimental routines at the Kling Klang studio when Schneider tested a new gadget.[37]

Strictly adhering to the credo that function dictates form, the 'lyrics' offer only what is promised by the title, namely the repeated recital of the numbers from one to eight (in different languages). To this end, Schneider simply used a hand-held language-translator device built by Texas Instruments to provide the vocals. The visuals that accompany live performances of the track today match the music perfectly, as the recited numbers are projected on screen in time with the music. 'Numbers' often serves as the opening song for Kraftwerk concerts, as it encapsulates the guiding aesthetic ideas that Kraftwerk derived from the Bauhaus movement, in a pumping proto-techno nutshell.

Kraftwerk's recourse to a great German modernist tradition can be seen as redemptive work: an attempt to fulfil a potential that never had a chance to develop, cut short as it was by fascism. Something was missing. Therefore, backwards was the only way to the future, as Hütter explained: 'We all felt very lost. To be able to feel any bonds at all, we had to go back to the Bauhaus school. It sounds strange but to continue into the future we had to take a step back forty years. The Bauhaus idea was to mix art and technology. An artist is not an isolated creature that creates for the sake of creation, but as part of a functional community. In the same way, we are kind of music workers. The Bauhaus in electronic sounds.'[38]

Computer World:
Tomorrow's Music, Today

Retro-futurism doesn't concern itself solely with the tension of past and future as expressed in the anticipation of advanced forms of technology. It also explores the alienating and empowering effects these will have on our lives. A case in point is Kraftwerk's prophetic *Computer World*. Released in May 1981, it predicted the technological future that is our digital present with surprising accuracy. Without any doubt, it is Kraftwerk's most futuristic album. Concluding their amazing seven-year run of groundbreaking albums (from *Autobahn* onwards), *Computer World* is a milestone in the history of pop music.

The album was arguably Kraftwerk's most cohesive piece of work yet. Three years in the making, it went on sale shortly before the first personal computers came on the market. IBM launched the rather expensive 5150 model in August 1981; Commodore launched the more affordable Commodore 64 – the first true home computer – in August 1982; Apple, meanwhile, launched their first Macintosh in January 1984 – all within three years of the release of *Computer World*. The simple lyrics to 'Home Computer', written by Florian Schneider, were as topical as it got: 'I programme my home computer/ Beam myself into the future'.

Coming after the complex image adorning the cover of *The Man-Machine*, the artwork for *Computer World*, by Emil Schult, was slightly disappointing.

It showed a console featuring a monitor (on which simple depictions of the band members were to be seen, accompanied by the band name and album title), as well as a keyboard. As with *Radio-Activity*, the desk-top shown was an artistic impression of what a computer looked like and not a recognizable model.

Schneider at the time owned an SWTPC 6800 computer made by the Southwest Technical Products Corporation, and Schult took this as a model. Ironically, he used this machine exclusively for his speech-synthesis experiments. No computers were employed in the production of *Computer World*; the album was recorded with analogue equipment, but this only underlines its visionary power. In preparation, the band visited the Düsseldorf branch of IBM to learn first-hand the workings of digital technology. The visit proved decisive, as it convinced Hütter and Schneider that analogue technology would soon be outdated because of the superior benefits digital signal processing would bring in terms of speed, reliability and the increased potential to manipulate sounds.

Those listening to the English-language version of the album regrettably miss out on how detailed Kraftwerk's predictions of a future dominated by computing devices fitted with microprocessor technology were. The German version of 'Computerwelt' features a stanza that has no equivalent in the English lyrics to 'Computer World':

> *Automat und Telespiel*
> *Leiten heut' die Zukunft ein*
> *Computer für den Kleinbetrieb*
> *Computer für das Eigenheim.*

> (Coin-op video games and home consoles
> Introduce us to the future
> Computer for the small business
> Computer for the home.)

With an uncanny soothsaying quality, *Computer World* also prophesied that computers would have a role in our love lives. 'Computer Love', with its seductive melody, foretold the manifold opportunities the internet now provides, be it for romantic or erotic ends: 'Another lonely night/Stare at the TV screen/I don't know what to do/I need a rendezvous'.

If 'futurism is sometimes called a "science" bent on anticipating what will come, retrofuturism is the remembering of that anticipation';[39] this definition holds particularly true for *Computer World*. When we listen to this remarkable album today, we hear the visionary image of a bright future that our present reality has never managed to live up to. To return to

'Computer Love', we now know that the internet's manifold possibilities to connect people don't satisfy our true emotional needs as human beings. The song in fact presciently captures a degree of sadness and alienation in envisaging a scenario of personal isolation: a future saturated with technology but lacking in emotional connection. Only now can we fully comprehend that *Computer World*'s promise was an ambivalent one.

As Bussy correctly points out, 'lost on many was that the album was as much a warning about the dangers of a "computer world" as it was a celebration of the micro-technology that had brought computerization into people's everyday lives'.[40] With *Computer World*, Kraftwerk not only displayed a remarkable degree of foresight in predicting a human future based on computer technology but, crucially, backed this up with an uncompromising and crisp musical vision of the emerging sound of the future.

'Numbers', according to Alexei Monroe, was a 'successful attempt to define a new sonic aesthetic, directly inspired by the then small flow of numerical data'.[41] In view of the victory march of the financial sector in a liberalized economy, the track, with its obsessively repeated numeric sequences, carries a considerable dystopian quality: 'In our present context, the track brings to mind the massively disruptive automated trades and high-speed money transfers that accelerate and proliferate as austerity degrades the offline life conditions of entire continents.'[42]

Similarly, given the numerous revelations surrounding British and US government surveillance operations which have illegally intruded into the privacy of the public by monitoring phone calls or spying on email conversations, the dystopian mood of *Computer World* seems even more chillingly prescient. Kraftwerk correctly foresaw the near-totalitarian control computer technology would exert over our lives and its immense potential to wield power over society. As well as (what used to be) Germany's biggest financial institution, Deutsche Bank, the English-language version of 'Computer World' refers to policing agencies (Interpol, FBI and Scotland Yard). The original German lyrics add two further state bodies to the list: 'Inland Revenue and BKA [*Bundeskriminalamt*, i.e. Federal Crime Agency]/Have our data available'.

The last line is particularly apt: referring to the availability of personal data in a digital format, Kraftwerk predicted the computerized government intrusion into our privacy in the future computer world. But there is a historical background to this: Kraftwerk's wariness towards instruments of social control can be attributed to the German experience of both the totalitarian fascist regime under Hitler and the dictatorial communist system of the East German Democratic Republic.

Depicting a Nazi radio set on the cover of *Radio-Activity* was a clear yet implicit signal that subsequent governments still placed great importance on the control of the population. The disciplinarian reach of the Nazi apparatus and the East German secret police (Stasi) were strong enough already but, as Hütter and Schneider sensed, the introduction of a computerized means of surveillance would be a game-changer, giving the authorities even more powerful instruments with which to police the population.

The latter, in fact, was already a reality when Kraftwerk wrote the album. In the late seventies, the *Bundeskriminalamt* introduced the new technique of *Rasterfahndung* (dragnet investigation) to locate wanted terrorists in the Baader-Meinhof Group. The widespread paranoia at the time among a German public in fear of left-wing terrorism sanctioned this innovative form of computer-aided database analysis. Its success, however, was rather limited and, ultimately, prone to error.

Apparently, the apartment of Florian Schneider was once raided erroneously by anti-terrorist police who believed it to be a terrorist hide-out;

the band were also stopped and searched at road-blocks intended to intercept terrorists. On at least one occasion, the police were delighted to discover that they were not facing political extremists but the group Kraftwerk, with whom they were familiar.[43]

These police measures – also employed against environmental and anti-nuclear activists – generated considerable unease among many liberal Germans. Hütter and Schneider, too, must have dreaded the dystopian prospect of government agencies collecting and analysing the data of innocent citizens on a large scale. In a promotional interview for the album, Hütter explicitly spelled out Kraftwerk's stance on the matter with uncharacteristic political fervour.

Computer World, he said, is an artistic attempt to alert their listeners: 'By making transparent certain structures and bringing them to the fore-front – that is a technique of provocation. First you have to acknowledge where you stand and what is happening before you can change it. I think we make things transparent, and with this transparency, reactionary structures must fall.'[44]

Indeed, the issue of transparency (and account-ability) around government's acquisition of their citizens' personal information remains a strongly contested democratic issue, now more than ever. The extent to which West Germans at the time felt uneasy about state control over their personal data was vividly demonstrated in 1987 in the protests against the *Volkszählung*. The national census was the first such exercise in the Federal Republic and many Germans saw the collection of personal data as the advent of computerized state control. The massive movement to boycott it successfully persuaded a considerable part of the population to either falsify data or straightforwardly refuse to answer the rather harmless questions on marital status, religion, housing, employment status and nationality.

The census gathered only a fraction of the personal information people now willingly share on social media sites. Truly, the future that is today's world panned out differently from both the pessimistic and optimistic projections of 1981. The advent of the internet was a development not foreseen by Kraftwerk: the very backbone of our information societies plays no role on *Computer World*. However, the lyrics of 'Antenna' from *Radio-Activity* can be seen as a description of the state of mutual connectedness and constant interchange of information made possible today by the internet: 'I'm the transmitter/I give information/You're the antenna/ Catching vibration'.

Kraftwerk's website is testament to the ambivalence with which the band treats the demands of the internet age. Launched only in the late nineties, by which time most other bands already had a presence on the Web, it has kept to its minimalist, simple design and outdated feel. With obsolete bitmap fonts and primitive pixel animations, it consciously lags behind the standards expected in contemporary Web design. This is not just a retro-futurist statement but also seems to convey the message that Kraftwerk do not want to join in the online marketing game that other bands are pursuing.

Kraftwerk's Retro-Futurism and German National Identity

Chris Petit's road movie *Radio On* (1979) is a film that anyone even remotely interested in Kraftwerk should watch. The protagonist, investigating the suicide of his brother, drives from London to Bristol, through the English landscape, past ugly modernist architecture. Kraftwerk's music plays a special role in the film, which impressively anticipates the bleakness of post-punk Britain before the dawn of the Thatcher era. Early on, the viewer encounters a handwritten manifesto which obviously refers to Kraftwerk: 'We are the children of Fritz Lang and Wernher von Braun. We are the link between the twenties and the eighties. [. . .] Our reality is an electronic reality.'

This (adapted) statement, derived from an interview with Ralf Hütter, indicates a crucial artistic point of reference for Kraftwerk. Like David Bowie or Ian Curtis, albeit for different reasons, they searched for inspiration from the fruitful period that was Weimar Germany. Hütter and Schneider's aim was to rework the innovative pre-war culture in the post-war period. Unlike the British musicians, Kraftwerk, as Germans, had a further agenda: they wanted to overcome the disaster of Nazism in order to rebuild a continuum of avant-garde cultural development.

Kraftwerk scholar Pertti Grönholm sees Kraftwerk's retro-futurism as 'an attempt to bridge the gap, to reconnect progressive German culture of the post-war years to the damaged continuum of German culture, especially the legacy of the avant-garde of the 1920s and early 1930s'.[45]

Kraftwerk were, in this sense, the sons of great technological innovators such as Wernher von Braun and visionary pioneers in the arts such as Fritz Lang. It was in the pre-war period that Kraftwerk found both their intellectual and their artistic roots. These points of reference were very different from the critical counterculture that had developed after the 'student revolution' of 1968, which was more grounded in drug experiences, socialism or identification with the political struggle of countries in the developing world. The grand goal of the Kraftwerk project was updating the pre-war legacy in the increasingly consumerist society of West Germany in the seventies, a society which, though complacent, had been shaken by the traumatic experience of left-wing terrorism which culminated in the events of the German Autumn in 1977.

As Grönholm puts it, stressing the contemporaneous function of their retro-futurism: 'The Kraftwerkian rediscovery and revival of the past futures of the early 20th century was not primarily in order to predict or envision the future. Rather, Kraftwerk constructed a cultural and historical space that worked as an imaginary, both utopian and nostalgic refuge in culturally stagnated West Germany.'[46]

Kraftwerk considered their present in the seventies to be a cultural void: a transitory, interim grey zone framed by a terrible past fraught with nationalist excess. Between genocide and a brighter future inaugurated by a post-war generation that had learned its lessons from a terrible history, Kraftwerk reanimated the trust of past avant-garde movements in the liberating, beneficial potential of technology – though without neglecting its inevitably dangerous aspects.

How Kraftwerk gave expression to the notion of the present being a void can be seen in the retro-futurist video to 'The Model', a pop song which sounded futuristic to listeners not yet fully attuned to electronic music yet featured black-and-white catwalk scenes in which models wore old-fashioned couture. The disjunction is deliberate: there is a friction between the futuristic soundtrack and their retro outfits.

Furthermore, amid the vintage footage, there is a short sequence showing a model wearing a futuristic outfit that evidently cites the sartorial aesthetics of *Raumpatrouille Orion* (*Space Patrol Orion*). This was the first German science-fiction series to be broadcast on television, in autumn 1966, in black and white. Comprising seven episodes, this German precursor to *Star Trek* was a huge success and retains its cult status in Germany even today.

The futuristic soundtrack by the Peter Thomas Orchestra, with its innovative sounds fusing beat music and jazz played by an orchestra, must have appealed to Kraftwerk.[47] Viewers of 'The Model' video would hence see both outdated and futurist outfits – but no contemporary models wearing couture from the early eighties, even though the song was clearly about the phenomenon of the 'super-model'.

Around the Globe: The *Computer World* World Tour of 1981

The release of *Computer World* brought with it the difficult issue of how to tour and perform the landmark album live. The most recent Kraftwerk concerts had been to publicize *Radio-Activity* in the autumn of 1976, a short European tour that closed with three dates in the UK (Sheffield, Coventry and the London Roundhouse). During their five-year absence from the stage Kraftwerk released no fewer than three milestone albums – *Trans-Europe Express*, *The Man-Machine* and *Computer World*; it was the most densely productive period of their career.

The world was eager to hear Kraftwerk's genre-defining music live, at long last. To meet this demand, the band transformed the Kling Klang studio set-up by reconfiguring their equipment into modular form. The various music machines and pieces of electronic equipment, originally designed to function as independent units, were now connected with each other, allowing the band a much greater level of control and to streamline their operations. This was an arduous task and took three years to complete. The declared aim was to enable Kraftwerk to take the entire set-up on tour.

And so they did, as this was the only way to replicate the increasingly complex musical production of these three albums in a live setting. Hütter explained: 'It took a lot of work to make the Kling Klang studio transportable, to really stage it, to install it in situation. All the parts are connected, it's a new conception of Kraftwerk: before it was studio plus live, now it's live studio, we play the studio on stage.'[48]

This feat located Kraftwerk not just aesthetically but also technically at the forefront of developments in the live performance of electronic music. They were not only pre-empting later stage practices in electronic music, they also put the Kling Klang studio on display, making the spectacle of the music machines a part of their show. The line between their everyday workplace and the stage as a temporary, special space created and inhabited only for public appearances was dissolved.

Embodying the man-machine concept included being mostly motionless on stage, to mark them apart from standard rock acts: 'Our rather static performance is necessary for emphasizing the robotic aspect of our music.'[49] However, as part of Kraftwerk's calculated efforts to subvert established boundaries, even their own, during the playful encore section the band members would leave their positions and come to the front of the stage holding everyday-gadgets-turned-Kraftwerk-gear, such as a Bee Gees-themed keyboard from Mattel, a drum trigger pad or a Stylophone. They would often use this opportunity to make direct contact with the audience, allowing people in the front row to initiate the sounds themselves.

'Kraftwerk made a performance out of their working environment, and they did so at a time when the working world was itself beginning to change.'[50] Kraftwerk not only proclaimed themselves 'music workers', they also brought their mobile workplace with them, as it were, allowing the audience to watch them operate their machines, in pretty much the same way as people today bring their laptops to work in cafés and other public spaces. The spectacle of seeing Kraftwerk playing live became a confirmation that the computer world had indeed arrived – Kraftwerk seemed to have fallen directly out of the future.

The positioning of the musicians and their machines on stage formed yet another aspect of their performance. The *Computer World* tour, which began in May 1981 and lasted until the end of the year, introduced the new stage design: an inverted V-shape. Both the left and the right row consisted of four double and two single units each. Hütter and

Schneider would take their positions on the left and right side, respectively, framing Flür and Bartos, who stood in the middle.

This set-up allowed each musician to communicate with their fellow band members through eye contact while playing their instruments, but also meant they could see the audience. The intention of Hütter and Schneider was to style the stage to look like a laboratory, as Karl Bartos remembers: 'They wanted to have some kind of musical laboratory and make the consoles look very scientific.'[51]

The stage lighting accorded the music machines the same degree of importance as the band members, and towering over the musicians were four screens at the very back of the stage. Kraftwerk had by now moved away from basic slide-show projections to video visuals, upgrading to four large Sony video screens, one behind each band member. Each screen would show the same image, emphasizing the notion of uniformity so crucial to the band's identity. In line with this, the new dress code for the stage saw every band member clad in identical outfits.

Considerable effort had gone into producing the video material and trying to synchronize it with the music. From the beginning, Hütter and Schneider had envisaged creating 'musical paintings'; the process of merging the music with its visual counterpart began in the eighties. It has now lasted for three decades, culminating in today's 3D visuals. 'Video can say more,' Hütter explained in 1983. 'During the concerts, we want the videos we show to enlarge our music, increase its prophetic and visionary side.'[52]

Slide shows were used for concerts from around the mid-seventies, but from the *Computer World* tour onwards, Kraftwerk performances featured video material exclusively as the visual complement. The videos combined stills, archive footage, graphics and excerpts from their promotional videos. Over the course of the years, and from tour to tour, the visuals became more important and sophisticated. (One advance from the *Computer World* tour to *The Mix* tour a decade later was the neat synchronization of visuals and music, as Kraftwerk could now control the projections more reliably via Atari computers.)

The arduous world tour, which comprised some ninety dates on four continents, set the standard format for future Kraftwerk shows up to 1998: mood-setting electronic noises played while the audience entered the venue, the Votrax speech synthesizer greeted the audience in German and introduced the band as 'Kraftwerk – die Mensch-Maschine', and then came a set that almost always started with 'Numbers' and later featured the first-generation 'robots' on stage during their theme tune. At the time of the *Computer World* tour, these were still the immoveable dummies first used at the press launch of *The Man-Machine* in 1978.[53]

There were small changes to staples such as 'Autobahn', to which a few new lines of lyrics were playfully added. Still, this hardly amounted to the improvisational aspect that had characterized the first few years of their stage performances. Previous live favourites, such as the staple 'Ruckzuck', had now vanished from the set. Indeed, after 1976, no songs from the first three albums would be performed live.

This underlines the sense that something crucial was changing for Kraftwerk in 1981: the structured approach that had become ever more important in the Kling Klang studio during the latter half of the seventies was now reflected in their stage practice. This was to reinforce the Kraftwerk concept centred on the idea of the man-machine, leading to an increasing rigidity that has characterized the format of Kraftwerk live shows ever since.

The band were pleasantly surprised when many audience members started to dance when they played tracks from their three most recent albums (*Trans-Europe Express*, *The Man-Machine* and *Computer World*). 'Just as Kraftwerk had straddled the barrier between improvisational music and electronic pop, now they had secured the bridge between electronic pop and dance music.'[54]

Hütter singled out one specific audience: 'We have always played in different situations, in different countries, different cultures,' he said, but 'when we were playing in America, there was always a large part of the audience which was dancing: the black audience, Hispanic, Hispano-American, etc. [. . .] Electronic music is really a world language, it is the music of the global village.'[55]

Playing their music literally across the globe – in Eastern and Western Europe, Japan, Australia, India and America – the tour provided a kind of feedback on the cultural shifts that had taken place in the seventies: not just the victory march of electronic music, but also the international dimension of the new sounds and the subsequent yet unexpected cultural fusions, of which the band, holed up in their Düsseldorf studio for half a decade, had been largely unaware.

The *Computer World* tour showed Kraftwerk at the top of their game. It concluded on 14 December 1981 with a show in Oyten near Bremen. A few months later, 'Planet Rock' by Afrika Bambaataa & The Soulsonic Force was released, OMD had the first of a string of million-selling hits vastly informed by the Kraftwerk sound, Depeche Mode were gearing up to become the mega-act they are now and the New Romantics in London danced the night away to Kraftwerk tunes played by DJ Rusty Egan.

Wherever you looked, the musical footprint of Kraftwerk was discernible. Fittingly, it was in February 1982 that 'The Model', originally released in 1978, began its climb to the number-one spot in the UK singles charts. The increasing availability and affordability of electronic music machines made it much easier to pick up from where Hütter and Schneider had worked very hard to arrive.

The band must have viewed this development, testament to their visionary power to change the course of pop music, with a mixture of delight and trepidation. Perhaps in response, it was during this period that they took up cycling, obsessively. Digitalizing the degrading analogue tapes was another such evasive manoeuvre. There would be no more concerts for another eight years, and it would take a full five years before a new studio album was released, after a prolonged, painful gestation.

5. ENTER THE DIGITAL REVOLUTION: FROM *TECHNO POP* TO *TOUR DE FRANCE*

Peter Boettcher

Robots at Cité de la musique, Paris, in September 2002.

The Difficult Road to
Electric Cafe/Techno Pop

The successor to *Computer World*, initially called *Techno Pop*, had already been recorded by 1983. It was even advertised in the German music business magazine *Der Musikmarkt*, complete with cover artwork and catalogue number. The artwork showed a peloton of four cyclists, now familiar from the (later) *Tour de France* album, against a plain beige background. Hütter had seen the motif showing two cyclists on a Hungarian stamp from the fifties and adapted it for Kraftwerk's purposes.

But then Hütter and Schneider decided to scrap the album. Some songs can now be found on the internet; it is easy to see why they were unhappy with the first version of *Techno Pop*. The tracks sound bland and somewhat boring, lacking that extra punch later versions possess. Reliable information is thin on the ground, but it appears that there are no 'left-overs' from the original *Techno Pop* album in the vaults, as all the material was reworked for the new version, released in 1986 under the title *Electric Cafe*.[1]

Hütter was involved in a cycle accident in 1983, and this was another factor that prolonged the genesis of the successor to *Computer World*. Reports about this incident vary greatly; while Hütter himself always insists that the accident left him in hospital for only a few days, other accounts mention serious injuries and that he was lucky to have returned from a coma. During this period Kraftwerk also decided to catch up musically with their competitors by going digital. For the first time, new digital technology was used predominantly for the recording process, although the finished product was still recorded on analogue master tapes.

More than with *The Man-Machine* and *Computer World*, Hütter and Schneider relied on external help with the production of this difficult album. Salvation was sought from various US producers for mixing and mastering; the list of collaborators included the then up-and-coming house producers DJ François Kevorkian and Ron Saint Germain, while the final mastering was carried out by the renowned Bob Ludwig, who had worked with Jimi Hendrix, Bryan Ferry and Bruce Springsteen. The protracted production process therefore necessitated several flights across the Atlantic. Hütter was not happy with the initial results, which caused further delays. But it was in Kevorkian's studio that Hütter first saw a digital Synclavier system in action when producing the mix for the single 'The Telephone Call'. (This would spark a momentous decision that was to have significant repercussions for the Kraftwerk story.)

They finally released *Electric Cafe* in November 1986, but the dawn of the digital era began badly for Kraftwerk. As it had been a full five years in the making, many Kraftwerk fans expected more from the album. So far, it was the longest gap between any two Kraftwerk albums. (Little did anybody suspect that there would be another five-year gap before Kraftwerk released their next album.)

One source of disappointment was that, unlike the albums from *Autobahn* to *Computer World*, *Electric Cafe* did not feature a convincing concept. The innovative spirit that was the hallmark of previous Kraftwerk albums seemed to have evaporated. *Electric Cafe*, on first listen, gave the impression of being little more than a supplement to the series of masterpieces that were released in quick succession from 1974 to 1981.

In contrast to this negative assessment of the album, techno scholar Sean Nye has convincingly argued for the album to be reassessed following the decision to reinstate the original title, *Techno Pop*, with the release of the *Catalogue* box set in 2009.

As Nye argues, the record must be included in the series of concept albums, since the name change makes it an explicitly self-reflective album about genre constructions and the pop success of electronic music.

Specifically, the title refers to the eighties 'techno pop' movement, a predecessor to the more well-known techno post-1989, a development in dance music that Kraftwerk had helped to generate. As Nye writes: 'In this case, Kraftwerk reflects the 1980s discourse of the genre of technopop (a variation of synth-pop and forerunner to techno), by splitting technopop into the musical concept album of *Techno Pop*.'[2]

The album can be understood as Kraftwerk's attempt to stake their claim in the world of electronic pop music which they had ushered in by appropriating the genre term 'techno pop' and updating the concept of *industrielle Volksmusik*. Unlike the latter, however, they cannot claim to have invented the term. The British band The Buggles, a duo composed of Geoffrey Downes and Trevor Horn (who later rose to fame as a hit producer), had a B-side entitled 'Technopop' backing their 1980 single 'Clean, Clean'.

In Japan, the Yellow Magic Orchestra had developed their own distinctive style of synth-driven pop music which was often dubbed techno pop. 'Japanese technopop is poised to invade America,' claimed *Rolling Stone* magazine in 1980.[3] In France, Kraftwerk ally Paul Alessandrini used the term to describe their music, and this may have inspired the band to make it their own.[4]

Having scrapped the first, analogue-recorded version of the album in 1983, Kraftwerk worked on the new, largely digitally recorded final version from 1984 to 1986. The eighties were not easy for Hütter and Schneider. Wolfgang Flür left the band first, due to long periods of artistic inactivity, followed by Karl Bartos in 1991. *Electric Cafe* was Flür's last Kraftwerk album. He became increasingly frustrated that Hütter and Schneider stayed away from the Kling Klang studio, preferring to cycle, a pursuit Flür hated.

As for Bartos, his decision to quit was to some extent motivated by reasons similar to those of Flür, but in addition there were musical differences. He was unhappy with the way in which the music was now being made. Bartos wanted to cling to the tried-and-tested style of working which relied more on improvising and playing together as a band. Hütter, however, fully embraced the new opportunity of working with digital studio technology, which allowed them to assemble the tracks through cutting and pasting, adding and moving samples along the chronological sequence.

Bartos also wanted more of a say in terms of the musical direction taken by the band and a fair recognition of his contributions, such as the riff he had composed for 'Sex Object'. *Electric Cafe* was the first and only Kraftwerk album to feature a song that was not sung by Hütter, namely 'The Telephone Call', which was written and sung by Bartos. (Perhaps unsurprisingly, the 2009 remastered version of the album retitled *Techno Pop* featured the shorter single edit of the track, which reduces the vocals by Bartos and hence his presence in the Kraftwerk œuvre.)

Another vocal oddity is the female synthetic voice on 'Musique Non Stop',[5] which was modelled by Schneider on the real voice of the American computer artist Rebecca Allan. She was drafted in by Hütter and Schneider to create cover artwork based on digital graphics, corresponding to the digital sound of the album. New York-based Allan was the pre-eminent figure in the field of computer-generated images at the time, a technology that is now part and parcel of video and film production.

In a painstaking process that took several months, she produced the polygonal likenesses of the faces of Hütter, Schneider, Bartos and Flür for the once path-breaking but now decidedly retro-futurist-looking design of the album artwork.

More importantly, the digital modelling of the band members' faces served as the basis for the video to 'Musique Non Stop'. As Ralf Dörper, keyboardist of Düsseldorf band Propaganda and member of Die Krupps, said: 'That Kraftwerk video clip shaped the MTV era, and it became the anthem of the music channel. MTV didn't hesitate to put it on heavy rotation to identify itself massively with the message: Music Non Stop.'[6] At the time, the effect on viewers was stunning: the faces simultaneously looked both recognizable and artificial. There is a particularly uncanny moment in which the computer-generated animated face of Schneider suddenly opens his eyes and sings: 'Music non stop'.[7]

It might seem odd that the title track, 'Electric Cafe', was originally to be found at the very end of the album; in addition, this fairly short track was not particularly interesting in musical terms. David Buckley notes the remarkable similarity to the melody of 'Trans-Europe Express'.[8] It is not entirely clear what Kraftwerk meant when they imagined an electric café in the multilingual song – the lyrics certainly don't have anything to do with an establishment serving food and beverages.

The French (and Spanish) lyrics describe the

sound of techno pop in the atomic age: 'Musique rythmique/Son électronique/L'art politique/À l'âge atomique'. It is sometimes argued that Kraftwerk predicted the rise of internet cafés as an early step in the digitalization of our society, but the lyrics certainly don't allow such a reading. In line with the (somewhat hidden) concept of the album, 'Electric Cafe' represents meta-music: (electronic) music about (electronic) music.

This in particular applies to the suite of tracks that occupies the A-side: 'Boing Boom Tschak', 'Techno Pop' and 'Musique Non Stop' form the conceptual core of *Electric Cafe*. The three tracks are the centrepiece and musical highlight of the album. As Nye has pointed out, the seventeen-minute suite can be compared structurally to the 'Trans-Europe Express' suite (which runs to a little under fourteen minutes). In both cases, the tracks both 'work individually and as one seamless mix',[9] with the suite encapsulating the central concept of the album.

Opening track 'Boing Boom Tschak' offers a playful take on the German literary tradition of sound poetry. The song toys with the nonsensical words of the title, whose sole purpose is their funny sound. Evidently, these are derived from the ono-matopoeic language of comic books, making it yet another children's favourite in Kraftwerk's œuvre. Synthesized voices sighing a satisfied 'ahhhh' and a strict 'psst!' are added to the mix. This use of samples links the song to the hip-hop technique of beat-boxing, a form of vocal percussion mimicking electronic instruments, and to tracks such as the Art of Noise's experimental 1983 hit 'Beat Box'. In any case, it is a great opening to the suite.

Next up, with a running time of well over seven minutes, is 'Techno Pop', built around a deep, metallic drumbeat. The use of German, Spanish and English endows the lyrics with an international flavour, hinting at electronic pop music's worldwide success: 'Synthetic electronic sounds/Industrial rhythms all around/Music non-stop/Techno pop'. This is not just true in the sense that electronic music has indeed thrived and innovated ever since, it was also somewhat prophetic, given that Kraftwerk had by this time in 1986 already been in existence for sixteen years; little could even Hütter and Schneider have imagined that, three decades on, the band would still be touring the world to acclaim and continuing to release music.

Track number three, 'Musique Non Stop', concludes the suite by way of manically repeating the title words, driving home the message that 'techno pop', a.k.a. electronic pop music, was now unstoppable. The male and female android voices which sing-speak the lyrics originated from a voice synthesizer discovered by Schneider. The track has come to play a special role in the Kraftwerk canon: once the band resumed touring in the early nineties, Kraftwerk would conclude their concerts with the 'Techno Pop' suite, habitually (and not without a little irony) making 'Musique Non Stop' the closing track of their set. This performance ritual has been a fixture of most of their concerts since.

Each of the four band members demonstrates his skills and his part in the overall concert experience during the track: each has, as it were, a solo on his own equipment. Ralf Hütter, turning towards the others, nods and taps his feet to the beat as they exit the stage one by one, leaving him alone on the stage, working the keyboards, for the final minutes of each concert.

The last few seconds of each show are also the only time Kraftwerk address or acknowledge the audience; Hütter normally utters, 'Thank you and good night,' in the language spoken by the audience. Very rarely, if it is a particularly special location or event, he adds a few words. After all, the music has communicated all that needs to be communicated.

Enter the Digital Revolution

As Bartos details in his autobiography, Kraftwerk were somewhat overwhelmed by both the musical and the technical developments in electronic music in the eighties. Hütter saw salvation in digitalization and so acquired the necessary technological gadget – for a considerable amount of money – on a trip to the US in late 1986. In January 1987, the New England Digital Synclavier II (first encountered in Kevorkian's studio) arrived. This day proved to be a crucial turning point: Kraftwerk went digital.

The Synclavier II was a digital synthesizer and sampler with a 'direct-to-disk' option provided by floppy-disk drives. It was extremely powerful, with the capacity to record on sixteen tracks at high resolution, at least by the standards at the time. The machine was of considerable size and needed modifications to function properly in the Kling Klang studio, particularly with regard to its cooling systems. And there was one further problem with it: the Synclavier II was terribly difficult to operate.

It came with a number of complicated manuals, and training was required to use it to its full capacity. With Hütter and Schneider preoccupied with cycling, they needed a skilled studio engineer to look after and operate the machine. A suitable candidate, at the recommendation of Karl Bartos, was found in Fritz Hilpert.[10] His task was to familiarize himself with the complicated workings of this powerful machine and then to sample the old multitrack tapes in order to take Kraftwerk's music into the digital age.

At the same time, Hütter and Schneider asked sound engineer Joachim Dehmann to help them address some structural problems in the acoustics of the Kling Klang studio. It was unsuitable for mixing, which was now a priority, because it tended to swallow bass waves. In the course of the revamp, overseen by Dehmann, the speakers and mixing desk were repositioned, a new wiring system was installed and the soundproofing upgraded. The work was completed in January 1989. Together with the acquisition of the Synclavier II, which is said to have cost close to a million dollars, this represented a considerable investment on the part of Hütter and Schneider.

Both developments changed the character of the Kling Klang studio significantly – it became less a place where the band members would work on new music through improvisation and technical experimentation and more a place where engineers would work on their behalf on the 'music data'. With the move from analogue to digital, a new epoch had indeed begun for Hütter and Schneider.

Instead of working on a new studio album, they increasingly turned their focus to the sound design of the existing music, and this led to a corresponding change in personnel. With the musicians Flür and Bartos leaving, sound engineers and studio technicians such as Fritz Hilpert and Henning Schmitz moved in, not just to help with music production in the Kling Klang studio but also to join the live line-up. And while Flür and Bartos are most readily remembered as a vital part of Kraftwerk during the glory years between 1974 and 1986, their successors have subsequently served as (rather anonymous) employees of Hütter (and Schneider) for more than twice as long (so far).

The Mix as Watershed

The Mix, released in June 1991, may well be Kraftwerk's least-loved album. Today, it sounds dated, particularly when compared with the current live incarnations of the songs in this would-be 'greatest hits' package. Although easy to overlook, however, the compilation denotes a crucial watershed in the development of Kraftwerk's body of work. What it embodies, one could say, is a kind of reversal of artistic thrust: no longer driving forward the development of electronic pop music, Kraftwerk began to look back on their extraordinary œuvre in order to revisit, refine and revise it. Less future, more retro, if you like.

One can assess this reorientation in two ways. One could say that Hütter and Schneider realized they had been overtaken by their erstwhile imitators and followers, in particular British synth-bands OMD and Depeche Mode, as well as by more commercial acts like The Human League, Soft Cell and Duran Duran. They – rightly – saw no point in entering into a futile catch-up struggle with them. Another way to look at the matter, however, is to argue that Kraftwerk had successfully completed their mission to single-handedly revolutionize pop music so could now comfortably concentrate their efforts on updating and expanding on it as a constant work in progress.

This may sound a little cheesy, or even arrogant. But their albums were so far ahead of their time that when technology finally caught up with their vision, it would have been foolish not to make use of the opportunities it offered. New developments in hardware allowed them to engage with the 'software' of the 'music data' in different ways. As a result, linear progress gave way to a modus operandi that focused on retrospective elaboration, expansion and evolution.

Except for *Tour de France*, the only major releases after *The Mix* were the live album *Minimum-Maximum* and the two retrospective box sets, the remastered *The Catalogue* in 2009, and 2017's *3-D The Catalogue*, which documented live shows between 2012 and 2016. The seeds planted decades ago could now really begin to blossom, given the new technologies available: digital sound mixing, digital remastering, 3D video projection, live sound processing creating 'virtual' sound objects, to name just a few.

Following the release of *Electric Cafe* as their first digitally (and most stressfully) produced album, a presumably relieved Hütter and Schneider went back to cycling. There were no plans to embark on a tour, let alone a follow-up album. Fritz Hilpert, however, was working away on the Synclavier to digitalize Kraftwerk's back catalogue. With Flür already gone, Bartos lasted only a few years more, eventually leaving in the same year *The Mix* was released, deciding that the only way to pursue his own career as a musician was to say goodbye to Kraftwerk.

The loss of personnel and the extensive digitalization efforts of course meant major changes in the five-year aftermath of *Electric Cafe*, though these were barely visible to the outside world. The most evident result of these transformations was the release of *The Mix* in June 1991. Not everyone in the Kling Klang camp at the time was convinced by this new direction. Emil Schult expressed his concerns: 'I wasn't sure about *The Mix*. Would Leonardo da Vinci have taken the *Mona Lisa* back and painted her over? I guess not. "Autobahn" didn't need a remix by Kraftwerk.'[11]

The album did indeed lack any strong justification for its existence; it appeared to many fans like a gap-filling exercise. To avoid the impression that Hütter and Schneider would lower themselves to producing something as artistically trivial and commercially oriented as a Kraftwerk 'best of' package, their biggest hit, 'The Model', was conspicuously absent. Also, for the first time since *Trans-Europe Express*, the album artwork depicted only the robot-dummy likenesses of Hütter (on the front) and Schneider (on the reverse), indicating that Kraftwerk had essentially reverted to the duo of *Ralf and Florian*.[12]

The actual purpose of *The Mix* was to showcase up-to-the-minute digitalized sound quality. Contrary to common conjecture, the tracks weren't remixes but completely new digital recordings, based on sampled elements of the original analogue tapes. The revision process, as already discussed, also included updates of the lyrics – apart from adding the crucial 'stop' to 'Radioactivity', Hütter and Schneider also dropped the reference to meeting David Bowie and Iggy Pop at Düsseldorf station in 'Trans-Europe Express', probably because such name-checking sounded increasingly dated.

Some fans felt that these changes undermined the original work, but these concerns certainly didn't matter to Kraftwerk; Hütter and Schneider had deliberately set out to change their artistic direction by reworking the existing material with a view to updating it. Their new way forward was to look back, a disappointing yet simultaneously crafty move. Old tracks were now polished by adding innovative textures, novel ideas and fresh arrangements. The bpm of some songs was also bumped up to make the music more danceable, as the new version of 'The Robots' revealed. When it was released, *The Mix* sounded very much of its time, with evident nods to contemporary techno and house trends; yet, for the very same reasons, today the album appears somewhat dated, like so much electronic music from the early nineties.

Taken on its own, *The Mix* was only an intermediate step – the crucial game-changer for Kraftwerk's future history was indeed digitalization: 'We have transferred to digital all our sounds, all our memory, all the old tapes which were demagnetizing [. . .] Now all the Kraftwerk encyclopaedia is at our disposal, a complete catalogue.'[13] Hütter gave this explanation in 1991; few, probably, would have suspected that the course of Kraftwerk's development over the next three decades would be the curation of their own back catalogue (with the 2017 release of *3-D The Catalogue* live box set as the most recent incarnation).

The Mix, inadvertently and indirectly, inaugurated the second stage of the Kraftwerk story: a potentially never-ending, open process of constant improvement and adaptation. While the work in their first phase (1974–86) can be described as an update of modernist ideas in the retro-futurist mode, the second stage embodies a postmodern strategy of avoiding closure within a fixed work of art, in its stead representing it as a perpetually fluid work in progress. And that in turn necessitated the vital change in the locus of their artistic work, from recording new material in the confines of the studio to performing on stage.

The Mix Tour of 1991

From the early nineties, a new purpose for playing live emerged: no longer promotional tools for studio albums, concerts had become an end in themselves, demonstrating the sonically evolving nature of the Kraftwerk catalogue. We can now understand the tours as decisive stages in Kraftwerk's development as an artistic performance project.

The *Computer World* tour necessitated the transformation of the Kling Klang studio gear into portable stage equipment; now, the digitalization of the back catalogue was the precondition for taking live performances to a different level. This was first demonstrated on the thirty-five-date *The Mix* tour. 'We always change,' said Hütter. 'We don't feel bound to records. We take the concepts and go from there.'[14]

What fan testimonies describe as the most noticeable difference between *The Mix* tour and the *Computer World* tour was the sheer force of the digitalized sound and the pace of the concerts, with Kraftwerk seeming to perform constantly in fifth gear, thanks to now having all the sounds and sequences readily available at the press of a fingertip. The appearance of the 'robots' for the encore set was preserved from the previous tour, but the dummies had finally been updated to become the more impressive-looking models introduced on the cover of *The Mix*.

Now, there was added drama in their spectacular entry: for the first half of the song, a new 'The Robots' video was played on four screens on the dark stage, then these screens would disappear and reveal the new generation of dummies amid a flurry of flashlights. With their faces closely resembling those of the band members, black torsos and mechanical arms complete with life-like hands, these Kraftwerkian man-machines looked much more like real robots. They could now be seen moving their arms and heads, and also gained the ability to sway.

Another new feature, particularly in terms of Kraftwerk's live concert history, was the absence of Florian Schneider's electronic flute, which he played as late as the *Computer World* tour. One of the key features of Kraftwerk's original soundscape had disappeared for good.

Kraftwerk Reactivated: The Tribal Gathering Shows, Luton, 1997

Over the next few years, Kraftwerk would play only a handful of concerts each year, mostly at special events such as the Stop Sellafield benefit in Manchester (1992) and the Ars Electronica festival in Linz, Austria (1993). Their appearance at the Tribal

Gathering festival in May 1997 was a particularly significant occasion.

A crowd of about 35,000 ravers came together at Luton Hoo Estate for one of the largest electronic-dance-music gatherings ever, comprising both the big British acts at the time (such as Orbital and Paul Oakenfold) and major techno protagonists from Detroit (Carl Craig, Juan Atkins, Kevin Saunderson and Jeff Mills), as well as French copycats Daft Punk.

You could say that Kraftwerk were reaping what they had sown by headlining the bill. The response of the rave crowd was rapturous. Even the festival tent devoted to Detroit techno was vacated during the Kraftwerk show, as the audience and the DJs crammed into the main tent to see their German heroes playing live, in most cases for the first time.

Music critic Tim Barr, who attended the festival, wrote that Kraftwerk 'were the originators, the creative force whose innovations had inspired a whole new music, and more importantly, a whole new youth culture. To be in the audience at Tribal Gathering that night to see Kraftwerk was as much about a celebration of that culture as it was about the gig itself. Because of this, the show had a resonance far greater than that of a normal concert.'[15]

Premiering their dazzling fluorescent boiler suits (as well as their rather silly matching glasses),

the performance featured the four members standing in a straight line, emphasizing the impression
of order, uniformity and minimalism; it would
be the hallmark of their performances from 2002
onwards. (Kraftwerk would, however, use the
V-shape arrangement in 1993 and 1998.) Kraftwerk
ran through a sixteen-song set. A true surprise came
towards the end – the band played a new track of
about six minutes' duration, thumping techno with
a fast-paced beat and descending synth lines.

To this day, that piece, along with two other
instrumentals they played at Austrian and German
gigs in the same year, remains unreleased on record.
The tracks fuelled speculation that perhaps an album
has been put together that will never be released.
Judging by the quality of the three tracks that can
be found on the internet, this conjecture seems convincing, but it is unlikely that we will ever find out.
In any case, die-hard fans now attend every concert
possible just in case any new material is played on
stage. Their efforts, so far, have been in vain.

The Tribal Gathering performance seems to
have reinvigorated Kraftwerk's appetite for playing
live; in 1998, they toured Japan and the Americas,
as well as appearing at the Sónar festival in Barce-
lona and the Roskilde festival in Denmark. They
returned to Japan in December 2002, but also played

in Paris in September of that year. The high-profile shows at the postmodern Cité de la Musique venue marked another crucial step in the development of their performance history: laptops were used as a technical upgrade to reduce the amount of equipment necessary. Placed visibly on the console of each band member, this revamped look, employing the icons of mobile computing, further increased the visual sense of uniformity.

Fritz Hilpert explained the benefits of the technological leap forward: 'The reliability of the notebooks and software has greatly simplified the realization of complex touring set-ups: we generate all sounds on the laptops in real time and manipulate them with controller maps. It takes almost no time to get our compact stage system set up for performance.'[16] With the new set-up, they played a run of eight shows in Australia and New Zealand at the beginning of 2003, which also served as a warm-up for what was to come in 2004, following the release of the *Tour de France Soundtracks* album in August 2003.

Tour de France: 'Cycling is a dance of man and machine' (Hütter)

'Is an aptitude for cycling a prerequisite for joining Kraftwerk?' Ralf Hütter was asked in 2009. 'No,' he quipped, 'but it helps.' It certainly wasn't always the case. The obsession with cycling that gripped both Ralf Hütter and Florian Schneider started in the early eighties, with Schneider catching the racing-cycle bug first. Impressed by Schneider's light-weight chrome bike, Karl Bartos got a Koga Miyata model for himself, too, and Hütter followed suit.

Hütter and Schneider founded their *Radsport-gruppe* (literally, 'cycle sport group'), which was made up of friends and fellow enthusiasts, including Bartos and Emil Schult. Schneider rented a window-less basement room in an underground garage to be used as the headquarters. Hütter was particularly enthusiastic. He began to wear black cycling outfits and started shaving as well as oiling his legs to cut down wind resistance, as professionals do. Initially, as Bartos remembers, they did fairly short tours of some sixty kilometres, and talked about matters other than cycling. But once more people joined, things became more serious and even took an ideo-logical turn. And, crucially, cycling seemed to gain even more importance than work at the Kling Klang studio.[17]

Quizzed over their remarkable interest in cycling, Hütter explained: 'We are from Düsseldorf. We grew up near the borders of the Netherlands and Belgium. Cycling is part of our regional culture.

If we were from Southern Germany, it might have been different. Then we probably would have spent our time bob sleighing.'[18] The last remark was, hopefully, a joke at the expense of the interviewer. In any case, Kraftwerk opted for a pursuit that was the very antithesis of a rock'n'roll lifestyle: instead of sex and drugs and alcohol, they went for plenty of fresh air, healthy exercise and camaraderie with like-minded obsessives from outside the music business, including architects, barbers and medics.

Not that cycling is always a healthy pursuit: as mentioned, in 1983, Hütter suffered a severe crash; he was riding along the river Rhine, and allegedly not wearing a helmet. Still, looking at it from today's perspective, cycling certainly had a positive impact on Kraftwerk. For one thing, Hütter, now in his early seventies, seems to be fit and in shape to tour the world with the Kraftwerk live extravaganza. The decision to become a vegetarian and avoid alcohol, taken at the same time he took up cycling, probably helped, too.

In an interview with the Belgian entertainment magazine *Humo* in 2003, Hütter gave an insight into the extent of his cycling fixation: 'In the spring I cycled the Amstel Gold Race for cycling amateurs. I also never skip Liège–Bastogne–Liège, and each year there are some trips through the Pyrenees and Alps on my programme. [. . .] The whole ride: Col de Madeleine, Col de la Croix-de-Fer, Col de l'Alpe d'Huez, Luz Ardiden also and the Tourmalet. [. . .] I also did the Tour of Flanders a few times; very difficult.'[19] It appears that Hütter often spent five to six hours in the saddle a day; when on tour, he would sometimes be dropped at a distance of a hundred kilometres from the venue, to enable him to get his daily dose of cycling.

With star-struck awe, Hütter described how he took part in the 2003 centenary of the Tour de France, riding in a race car with the cyclist Gilbert Duclos-Lasalle: 'In such a car you are very close to the cyclists. [Enthusiastically] On a certain moment we drove along the car of Leblanc! The Tour manager! I haven't been so enthusiastic since my childhood. Of course, you cannot follow the race as well as on television, but you can smell and feel it. It was simply fan-tas-tic.'[20]

The first musical evidence of Hütter and Schneider's cycling mania came in 1983 with the release of the 'Tour de France' single, a taster from their ill-starred first version of *Techno Pop*. The single seemed to develop a life of its own, appearing in various modifications, two distinctive official videos (with at least four different versions) and recordings on various formats, both analogue and digital.[21]

The 2003 release of the *Tour de France Soundtracks* album was no less than a sensation. Kraftwerk were back, seventeen years after their last studio album. However, the band missed their target to coincide the release with the centenary of the Tour de France in July 2003 by a few days. (The album came out in early August.) At long last, Ralf Hütter's unrelenting promise that new material would be on the way and released as soon as possible seemed to hold true. While their previous studio effort, *Electric Cafe*, received mostly indifferent reviews, *Tour de France Soundtracks* went straight to number one in the German album charts – the first time one of their albums had reached the coveted top spot.

It was a remarkable success for the band, particularly given that only three years earlier Kraftwerk had been widely attacked in the German media for cashing in (to the tune of approximately 200,000 euros) by creating a four-second jingle for the Expo 2000 world fair held in Hanover. The short piece of music was denounced as no more than a 'cultured doorbell sound' while a representative of the German lobby group of taxpayers complained that the trade fair management had chosen a band which 'was known to the average member of the public, if at all, only peripherally'.[22]

Maybe in order to counter the worries of

concerned German taxpayers, Kraftwerk expanded the jingle to the full-blown track 'Expo 2000' which was released in various mixes on the *Expo 2000* EP in 1999. Retitled later as 'Planet of Visions', the song is now a staple of Kraftwerk shows. And maybe the subsequent release of an album after first stirring up some controversy was a good strategic move, reminding the German public that Kraftwerk were still going strong – and perhaps this explains in part the surprising chart success of the album.

It is perhaps a little odd that Kraftwerk followed the trajectory of car and train not with the aeroplane or even the spaceship but with the bike. Conceptually, as far as the gradual creation of an overarching work of art on the theme of man and technology goes, at first glance it doesn't make much sense. Yet, from their perspective, it was a logical progression. Hütter and Schneider's fanaticism for cycling arose by coincidence at a time when ideas for and the thrust behind a new concept album to follow on from *Computer World* had evaporated.

Since they were always looking for inspiration from the quotidian and the real-life world around them, a cycling-themed album represented the logical next step in developing their œuvre. Even the fact that the idea was then shelved, to be eventually released only some twenty years later, can be considered as prototypically Kraftwerkian, given their propensity to allow great lapses of time between album releases.

The choice of the bicycle as the theme of a concept album may seem less weird if one recognizes that Kraftwerk has always perceived means of transport as instruments, in line with their artistic concept of turning everyday technical noise into the sounds of electronic music: as mentioned earlier, 'The bicycle is already a musical instrument on its own.'[23] With *Tour de France*, Kraftwerk made an album that creates its own sound cosmos of clicking gears, whirring chains, beating hearts, hissing valves and panting.

Critics of *Tour de France* – and there are a few of them around – are wrong, I believe. What the album achieves is to translate the experience of cycling into music, transforming the physical exertion of pedalling into the kinetic groove of the tracks: 'Cycling is very close to Kraftwerk. Time, movement, clear thinking. Exactly the same balance we use for our music. On the bicycle, you listen to the wind and the rhythm of your breathing.'[24]

The Tour de France was an ideal thematic framework for the album concept: 'It's kind of like part of our culture, our cultural background,' explained Hütter. 'The Tour has been going for over a hundred years. It's a cultural institution.'[25] Also, it allowed Kraftwerk to make an album in French, picking up on the European spirit and the references to France in *Trans-Europe Express*. The Kraftwerk discography is thus bookended by the German car and the French bicycle, with the trans-European train network connecting them.

The use of older footage for the accompanying visuals clearly aims to evoke a 'clean' version of the cycling event, which has since become plagued with accusations of doping and commercialization; a time when the sporting ideals of fairness, friendship and community suggested in the lyrics of the title song were probably still valid:

> *Crevaison sur les pavés*
> *Le vélo vite réparé*
> *Le peloton est regroupé*
> *Camarades et amitié*

> (Puncture on paving stones
> The bicycle quickly repaired
> The peloton is regrouped
> Comrades and friendship)

Proof of Kraftwerk's attachment to professional cycling was the memorable concert they played in early July 2009 at the Manchester Velodrome. The state-of-the-art cycle track is the home of the Team GB cyclists who triumphed at the 2008 Summer Olympics in Beijing. As part of the Manchester International Festival, Kraftwerk played the British debut of the 3D show at the sports venue.

When 'Tour de France' came on, four members of the UK cycling team emerged from behind the stage and began to race around the audience and the band, delivering palpable evidence of the propulsive quality of Kraftwerk's music. (Hütter told an interviewer that he got up early next morning to join the British team for a training session, making the concert a memorable occasion for him as well.)

Tour de France concludes with a new recording of the eponymously titled single but opens with a suite of five seamlessly interconnected tracks, with 'Tour de France (2ᵉ Étape)' being the centrepiece. The sound and melody of the original single (which was borrowed from the opening section of Paul Hindemith's *Sonata for Flute and Piano*) are notably different in the 'Tour de France' suite.[26]

Commencing with the aptly titled, synth-driven 'Prologue', the three sleek variations 'Tour de France Étape 1/2/3' are organized around a cyclical hiss that emulates the sound of a freewheeling bike and creates a trance-like effect on the listener. Metronomic and minimal, the tracks show the influence of contemporary electronic-music styles by creating the feeling of a music constantly thrusting forward until the slowed-down coda of 'Chrono' is reached. In its entirety, the suite easily ranks as a junior partner to the epic journey of 'Autobahn' and the mighty metallic spectacle of 'Trans-Europe Express'.

The album offers six more tracks, among which are some of Kraftwerk's finest achievements, especially 'Vitamin' and 'Elektro Kardiogramm'. All are minimalist songs with reductive lyrics, mostly in French. As such, they add a distinct cluster of tracks to the body of Kraftwerk songs, often comprising lists of nouns that, on the sonic level, complement the use of German and English with the elegant sound of the French language.

'La Forme', also issued as an eleven-minute remix by Hot Chip in 2007, is a prime example:

Inspiration, expiration
Contraction, décontraction
Ventilation, rotation
Extension et flexion

Préparation, musculation

Concentration et condition
Régénération, relaxation
Hydratation, alimentation

La forme

This track sings the praises of physical fitness, a necessity for any cyclist, but it is really a description of the human body as a machine and its mechanical operations during the physical exertion of cycling. The pairing of words allows Hütter to sing about the symbiotic functions of the body in a way that mimics their contrasting nature.

'Aéro Dynamik' deals with a physical phenomenon that needs to be battled against (head wind is a major nuisance for cyclists); 'Titanium', on the other hand, praises the light alloys employed in the construction of professional bike frames: 'Carbone, aluminium/Vélo, titanium'. Kept minimalist, they are Kraftwerk songs *avant la lettre*: 'Just a few words of lyrics, mainly buzz words, key words, with stress on their sound, the sound of words, speech songs – an early form of rap, if you like,'[27] as Hütter described the essence of Kraftwerk songcraft in 2004. For this reason, the tracks don't just form part of the overarching concept of the *Tour de France* album but also belong firmly in the wider body of the Kraftwerk œuvre.

'Vitamin' stands out as the only at least nominally German song – the lyrics are reduced to a list of vitamins to be found in the food-supplement pills cyclists who don't resort to doping take to enhance their performance on two wheels. The sequence of the vitamins recited is not arbitrary but tweaked to create a rhythm from the German pronunciation of the words: 'Kalium Kalzium Eisen Magnesium/ Karbohydrat Protein A-B-C-D Vitamin'. What began with the lyrics to *Autobahn* – Kraftwerk proudly employing their native language for the first time in their work – is reduced on their final album to a mere list of chemical elements yet still derives an aesthetic surplus from the sound quality of the German words spoken in a clear, measured rhythm.

When asked about influences on Kraftwerk's music, Hütter is often keen to stress the importance of silence. *Tour de France*, in a way, also aims to work with the sounds of silence. Or, as Hütter expounded in more detail:

> The other thing with cycling is that when it's really going well, it's really silence. You just hear the wind. That's what gave the music its flow on this album. We know that from cyclists, when they listen to our music, they understand; they listen, and they understand how the music is composed. It's important when you move with your bicycle to listen to the environment, the surroundings, the wind and your own breath. At least that's the way we see this.[28]

Mirroring the increasingly minimalist nature of the lyrics on *Tour de France*, Hütter once gave the following concise definition of what Kraftwerk and their music are all about: 'Movement. Motion and emotion.'[29] Cycling was hence the ideal vehicle for a further musicalization of movement: 'We are very interested in the dynamics and the energy and the movement. The German word is *vorwärts*, forward – that's what you do with your bicycle. You move forward.'[30] In 2004, an interviewer asked Hütter what he was most proud of. 'That we are still here,' he replied, 'and that we are still moving forward.'[31]

As well as movement, the body is another key theme of the *Tour de France* album. A case in point for the incorporation of the human body in the man-machine aesthetic is 'Elektro Kardiogramm'. It is one of their key conceptual tracks in its dense combination of major themes. The lyrics demonstrate an extreme concentration:

Elektro Elektro Kardiogramm
Minimum-maximum
Beats per minute

In a self-reflexive turn, the words in the second verse generate maximum aesthetic value from minimal means. This track, too, features heavy breathing in the opening section but, as the title indicates, the bodily sound that takes centre stage here is the heartbeat – made audible through the help of an electrocardiogram.

'The beat you hear in "Elektro Kardiogramm" is my heartbeat during cycling,' Hütter said. 'We took medical tests I did over a couple of years, heartbeat recordings, pulse frequencies, lung volume tests, and used those tests on the *Tour de France* album. It's percussive and dynamic.'[32] It is this authentic sound – recognizable as a heartbeat yet sounding like a bass drum – that provides the rhythmic backbone of the track, running at a little over 60 bpm.

What we therefore hear is, in a very literal sense, the heartbeat of the Kraftwerk man-machine, which in a brilliant conceptual feat dissolves the distinction between the rhythms of electronic music and cardiovascular activity. When the bpm rate drops to zero, both party and life are over. But the utopian idea is that the beat goes on, for ever. Or to quote Hütter once more on the topic of cycling being a manifestation of the man-machine: 'It's about dynamics, always continuing straight ahead, forwards, no stopping. He who stops falls over. It's always forwards.'[33]

Tour de France Soundtracks
Tour (2004–5)

With a stunning new album under their belt, Kraftwerk embarked on their second world tour with an appearance in Helsinki on 6 February 2004. They launched *Minimum-Maximum*, their first official live album, in June 2005 in the midst of the tour; it compiled twenty-two tracks on two CDs, with recordings from shows across (mostly) European, American and Japanese venues.[34]

In terms of stage design, it was the first world tour to feature the sparse look that now characterizes Kraftwerk concerts: a slightly elevated platform, four plain consoles each featuring a laptop, and one huge screen covering almost the entire stage.[35] The dayglo suits made a return during the encore set, while for the main set the band adopted a more sober look featuring neat dark grey suits, red shirts and black ties, a visual nod to the iconography of *The Man-Machine*.

The tour consisted of three legs, about ninety concerts in total. As so often with Kraftwerk, we can only speculate whether the strain of the lengthy tour contributed to Florian Schneider's decision to leave the band. When Hütter was questioned about the departure of his long-term partner, he remained characteristically tight-lipped. All he was prepared to reveal in public about Schneider's recent participation was: 'He worked for many, many years on other projects: speech synthesis, and things like that. He was not really involved in Kraftwerk for many, many years.'[36]

Maybe the stress of touring was only one reason for his exit, perhaps set against the wider background of Hütter's decision, now that the *Tour de France* album had been released, to focus exclusively on the maintenance, upkeep and cultivation of the musical 'plants' that had sprung to life in the Kling Klang studio. Because this is exactly what happened.

Gone, all of a sudden, were the erratic breaks in their public presence; Kraftwerk embarked on their version of Dylan's Never Ending Tour by playing concerts across the globe more or less continually. With the absence of new studio material for the foreseeable future, presenting their audio-visual *Gesamtkunstwerk* live has become the *raison d'être* for the band – now truly and finally a pure performance-art project.

Without a reluctant Schneider, who played his last Kraftwerk concert on 11 November 2006 in Zaragoza, and because the laptop-based stage set-up made things technically easier, touring seemed to have become an attractive proposition for Hütter and his three employees. In 2008 and 2009, Kraftwerk played an impressive number of festivals around the world, mostly headlining but also acting as support band to Radiohead for a seven-date tour of South America. (A dream bill!)

6. SOUND AND VISION 3D: WORKING ON *THE CATALOGUE*

Kraftwerk live.

Q: Are Kraftwerk like Andy Warhol in music?
A: If you want to put it like that, yes.
                                                     – Ralf Hütter

The Wolfsburg Concerts

The three concerts played on 25 and 26 April 2009 at the Altes Heizkraftwerk in Wolfsburg, a German city dominated by its principal employer, Volkswagen, denote yet another important step forward in Kraftwerk performance history. The venue, a disused heat-and-power station that used to be part of the gigantic Volkswagen production plant, provided an appropriate location for the band to premiere something exciting: for the last six songs of the show, the visuals were presented for the first time in 3D technology, which required audience members to wear special glasses.

After this successful trial, the passive 3D projection technology developed by the German company Awater 3D was extended to the entire Kraftwerk show in 2011. The first full 3D appearances took place in mid-October in Munich, in conjunction with the first gallery exhibition of Kraftwerk at the

Lenbachhaus, where the 3D visuals for some songs could be admired outside the context of a concert. The importance of this move to a full-blown audio-visual art form cannot be overestimated: in the same way that the move to digitalization had changed their thrust from developing new music to refining existing material, the move to introduce 3D visuals opened a new chapter in the Kraftwerk story.

The focus was now on improving the live experience for the audience, creating an increased degree of immersiveness through the introduction of an innovative sound system. This allowed Kraftwerk to create 'virtual' sound objects that could be freely moved across the listening space for a truly immersive and spatial sound experience which far surpassed previously available surround-sound systems. Sound, too, had emancipated itself from the bi-aural stereo set-up of the PA and had become, as it were, 3D.

Kling Klang Concerts

How would Elvis have sounded as a septuagenarian stage performer? Difficult to imagine, of course – in all likelihood, like a very bad parody of himself. Michael Jackson might have fared better, but who knows? David Bowie, no question, would have been great; sadly, we shall never know. His mate Iggy Pop still delivers his full-power punk-rock animal show, now somewhat hampered by problems with his hip and his knees, as well as other ailments that come with crossing the Rubicon of being seventy. Ralf Hütter, however, looks pretty good in his *Tron*-style dayglo leotard stage wear. Certainly, when the earth-shattering bass detonations of 'Man-Machine' vibrate through the body, he seems a very cool septuagenarian.

Kraftwerk concerts are cutting edge in terms of technology. The impressive state-of-the-art 3D video projection technology in use since 2011 creates striking visual effects for every song they perform, and there's lots more optical gimmickry. For one thing, the projections make you want to grab the notes which float towards the audience from the car radio during 'Autobahn' or dodge the spiky nose cone of the space ship that seems to hit you right in the eye when 'Spacelab' is played.

The visuals, in turn, are complemented by a superb-sounding forty-channel sound system based on wave field synthesis (WFS), which was premiered in 2013 at their hometown concerts at the Kunstsammlung NRW. This advanced audio technology was invented by the Fraunhofer Institute research laboratories in Germany and uses a large amount of computational power to drive independently controlled speakers in order to create immersive audio spaces that go far beyond what is delivered by conventional surround-sound systems. Tech talk aside, the effects created by the Kraftwerk sound engineer are impressive: a precise sound across the spectrum, reaching down to low frequencies that truly make your body shake during the performance of 'Man-Machine' and 'Radioactivity'.

In a way, the introduction of the WFS sound system fulfilled an ambition that Kraftwerk had held from very early on in their career but could not implement as the appropriate technology was not then available. An early definition of the *Gesamtkunstwerk* idea provided by Hütter in 1975 focused only on the effect of sound in turning a Kraftwerk concert into a fully somatic experience: 'We've had this idea for a long time, but it has only been in the past year that we've been able to create what we feel is a loudspeaker orchestra. This is what we consider Kraftwerk to be, a non-acoustic electronic loudspeaker orchestra. The whole thing is one instrument. We play mixers, we play tapes, we play phasers, we play the whole apparatus of Kraftwerk. That's the instrument. Including the lights and the atmosphere.'[1]

This statement somewhat neglects the visual component of Kraftwerk. But with their work strongly based on the artistic principle of minimalism, Hütter and Schneider seem to have later grasped, on a more basic level, that sound and vision, music and image, constitute the two main meta-languages in this universe. Given that music is the movement of sound through time, its 'natural' companion is the moving image. On a more trivial level, it may well be that Andy Warhol's artistic stratagem to work with both film and music (in addition to the 'still images' of art) inspired Kraftwerk's multimedia explorations.

Similarly, the idea of marrying both artforms in the Kraftwerk concept of the *Musikgemälde* (musical painting) was born before the technology that would allow Hütter and Schneider to truly fulfil their artistic vision was available. The first step in elevating pop music and moving image into an art form was the advent of MTV in 1981, as it sparked the explosion of music clips. The artistic videos by Kraftwerk were a favourite on the channel, which played not only 'Musique Non Stop', which chimed with its remit, but also the videos to 'Trans-Europe Express', 'The Model' and 'Pocket Calculator', all of which proved popular.[2]

But already in the early eighties Hütter was one step ahead. He had an interest in another form of visual technology, namely 3D film projection, visiting screenings of 3D films at Düsseldorf cinemas with the band members. At the time, there was a 3D craze which particularly focused on horror and sci-fi movies, such as *Friday the 13th Part III* (1982), *Jaws 3-D* (1983) and *Spacehunter: Adventures in the Forbidden Zone* (1983). 3D technology seemed to be the future of cinema – though it proved to be a short-lived trend. But the (3D) bug had bitten: to develop a fully 'illustrated' show with 3D visuals for each and every song from their œuvre would be the ultimate goal for Kraftwerk, though still thirty years in the future. As so often, Kraftwerk had to wait until technology caught up with their artistic visions.[3]

Kraftwerk now always perform a two-hour set, admittedly shorter than the live shows delivered by artists such as Bruce Springsteen, The Cure or the late Leonard Cohen. But there never is a dull moment. No fillers, no boring songs from the latest 'comeback album'. Also, none of the masochistic pleasures of seeing Bob Dylan, or, in the past, The Fall, who either refuse to play the good songs or butcher them; purely, it seems, to torture their paying audience.

Kraftwerk gigs, on the contrary, are pure bliss: in a sleek staging of their *industrielle Volksmusik*, they present a succession of milestones of future music in pristine sound quality. It's an overwhelming experience of crystal-clear sound waves entering not just the ears but every cell of the listener. Said Hütter in 2017: 'Music creates vibrations, sonic waves, that directly enter your body. That is their power.'[4]

Kraftwerk concerts hit the audience with a music that exists in an odd, paradoxical continuum of time: already futuristic when first released some decades ago, it now sounds like 'real music, the music of our digital age' (Hütter) precisely because it is not 'new', even though it sounds thoroughly contemporary.

Furthermore, a Kraftwerk concert never follows the usual patterns of rock concerts, with audience interaction between songs or roadies entering the stage to adjust gear. Yes, they play an even spread of tracks from all of their albums, released over the course of thirty years, but the gigs are not just a more or less arbitrary succession of individual songs. Instead, a Kraftwerk concert has to be comprehended as a total musical-visual-theatrical event, documenting the artistic will to unify, simplify and integrate the live-show experience. The specific format of the shows has been successively developed over the decades and is adhered to with ritualistic determination while also allowing for some smaller deviations to keep things interesting and, indeed, alive.

Kraftwerk present an artistically devised musical theatre as part of their *Gesamtkunstwerk* fusing sound and vision, music and image. By 1978 Hütter had commented: 'We call our music acoustical films, and actually when we perform in concert there's the volume factor and also the reverb and the echo of the hall where we play, because the volume of the music really is only there when we perform live, and the presence of people in the room changes the music.'[5]

But there is more to this theatrical performance: Kraftwerk concerts are now likely to take place at venues not traditionally connected to pop music but to highbrow art: opera houses, museums, symphony halls, theatres, and so on. The choice of city or venue is often also a crucial component of the overall performance: playing shows as part of the Grand Départ of the Tour de France or at the Manchester Velodrome links the gigs to the cycling theme; picking the Neue Nationalgalerie out of all potential Berlin venues signals their affinity to the Bauhaus, as it was built by modernist architect Mies van der Rohe; or taking their concerts to Detroit, as a sort of homecoming, in view of the Düsseldorf–Detroit techno axis.

The minimalist stage will be bare, save for four identical consoles at which the uniformly dressed musicians will stand mostly motionless, operating their machines with a mixture of cool casualness and concentration. Even without the 3D visuals, the Kraftwerk stage set is a sight to behold, signalling a marked deviation from standard stage practice at pop or rock concerts: 'The usual detritus of performance (the mic stands, the cables, the amps) are hidden,' as David Pattie notes. 'All clutter discarded, no sweat, no effort.'[6]

Neither are there any roadies nor (visible) monitor speakers for the band, no feedback noise, no unexpected encores, no between-song banter with the audience, no set-lists on a piece of paper to steal as souvenirs and definitely no water bottles, let alone bottles of beer, the regular rock musician's concession to human bodily needs. Though this may strike some as clinical, this forced minimalism is yet another deliberately curated aspect of the Kraftwerk concept. As Hütter explained: 'Some people perform with their musical machines built up high around them in an impressive way. We prefer the low-profile image, bringing man and machine together in a friendly partnership of musical creation.'[7]

For the 2004–5 world tour to promote *Tour de France Soundtracks*, the uniform consoles featured four laptops.[8] For a number of years now, those laptops, too, have vanished from view, which makes what the four band members are actually doing even more unfathomable from an audience's perspective. The music, it appears, is created out of nothing.

However, fan footage taken at the Amsterdam shows in January 2015 allowed a peek at their hidden live rig. Each console consists of a variety of equipment – displays or control units, or modulators – that is to say, gadgets of all sorts on which the band members push adjusters and twist knobs, both virtual and real. Ralf Hütter's console looks the most conventional, with half of it taken up by a keyboard for playing the melodies.

The distribution of stage roles among the Kraftwerk members since Florian Schneider left has never been a secret. Hütter, positioned on the far left, takes care of the melodies and, of course, the vocals; Henning Schmitz, Kraftwerk member since 1991, is in charge of the bass lines. Studio engineer Fritz Hilpert, who joined the live line-up to replace Karl Bartos, is responsible for rhythm and percussion; finally, the far-right position previously occupied by Florian Schneider is now allocated to the video operator taking care of the 3D visuals. Since 2013 this role has belonged to Falk Grieffenhagen, who succeeded Stefan Pfaffe, who had looked after the video projections from 2008.

Idle accusations that the computers and

machines do all the work at concerts have been levelled against Kraftwerk from early on. It goes without saying that such suspicion originates in the line of thinking that values the supposed 'authenticity' of sweating rock musicians working their guitars above the coolness of keyboard-pushing musicians – suspicion which is of course regarded with contempt. Though it is reasonable enough that fans equate value with effort and musical virtuosity, the complexity involved in creating the Kraftwerk live sound should not be underestimated. The three band members producing the music have to play closely together while the 'video operator' has to precisely synch the visuals and the sound engineer operates the wave field synthesis mix.

The occasional mistakes made on stage, resulting from the wrong key being pressed or a missed entry, in any case undoubtedly confirm that the band indeed plays live. Also, the technical problems that beset some of the early concerts are not over by any means, as the complete breakdown of the back speakers at the concert at the Dresden Albertinum museum in early February 2018 confirmed.

Eight Nights at the Museum:
At the MoMA and Other Art Galleries

With the increased emphasis on the visual dimension of their stage shows, Kraftwerk gained more and more interest from curators and the visual-arts community. By 2005, the band had already appeared at the Biennale arts festival in Venice, at a lavish cinema on the Lido. But the announcement that Kraftwerk would play a retrospective of their core works over eight evenings at the Museum of Modern Art in New York caused a sensation.

The concert series dubbed *The Catalogue – 12345678* opened another new chapter in the stage practice of Kraftwerk. Evidently tied to the *Catalogue* box set released in 2009, the first instalment of the eight-concert residencies in April 2012 immediately sold out, not least as the atrium of the museum allowed for a maximum capacity of only approximately four hundred people.

Further retrospectives at major art institutions not normally associated with pop music were presented across the globe. Significantly, the second instalment of *The Catalogue – 12345678* series took place at the Kunstsammlung NRW, a museum in the heart of Düsseldorf, in January 2013. These concerts, held in the rectangular Grabbe room of the museum, were the first to feature sound projection based on wave field synthesis technology.

From 1991 up to the MoMA *Catalogue* retrospective, Kraftwerk had worked with quadrophonic sound technology, but ever since the Düsseldorf shows, the new surround-sound technology enabled listeners to experience the full breadth of sound, regardless of where they happened to be in the room. The results were breathtaking, creating a completely new, even more all-engulfing listening experience for the audience members.

The ability to create a spatial audio mix allowed for such '3D effects' as hearing the train during *Trans-Europe Express* approaching from a distance and subsequently rattling through the right-hand half of the room or, similarly, hearing bikes passing by from the left and the right, giving the impression that a peloton was about to cycle right through the room during 'Tour de France'. Wave field synthesis works particularly well in open spaces; at the Düsseldorf open-air concert to mark the start of the Tour de France 2017, the Morse code beeps of 'Radioactivity' seemed to twirl around one's head, while the bass was truly earth-shattering.

After the Düsseldorf premiere of the new sound system, the band had an eight-day residency in London, playing at the iconic, eight-hundred-capacity Turbine Hall of the Tate Modern in February 2013. The incompetent planning of ticket sales at the Tate caused their website to crash due to overwhelming demand. As with the restricted availability of tickets for the New York MoMA residency, this resulted in a lot of angry fans being unable to see the band. (Unknown to many of them, tickets at the Tate were available on the door each evening.)

The Art of Music – Kraftwerk and the World of Art

Ralf Hütter sees Kraftwerk as a continuously ongoing, life-long project: not just music non-stop, but also work non-stop. 'We never took a break,'[9] he claimed in 2004 when discussing *Tour de France Soundtracks*. The interviewer challenged him on this, pointing out that the public had scarcely seen any new material from Kraftwerk for seventeen years. Hütter countered: 'An art project doesn't need to maintain its presence in the music business. We have worked on our *Gesamtkunstwerk* and our stage show, on all aspects of design and presentation, the visual aspect, the computer graphics, the music data. [. . .] Our work, behind closed doors, in the Kling Klang studio, took the time it needed. We are just a quite small, autonomous group of artists.'[10]

Significantly, music receives only a passing mention in this fairly lengthy self-description. One could assume that Kraftwerk were running a design or an art studio. And indeed, it has become increasingly impossible to detach the acoustic from the visual in Kraftwerk's body of work. Their visual identity is not mere packaging; it is almost as important as the music. There are design considerations at work with Kraftwerk that go back to the very first album from 1970, even before they had established their central man-machine concept. Hütter may hence rightfully claim: 'Every aspect of our design and visual identity was decided solely by us; album covers, videos and so on. We have been multimedia from the beginning. And we always determined our artistic path ourselves.'[11]

The visual side of their *Musikgemälde* always played a crucial role and new technological developments had made it possible (and advantageous) to add to the *Gesamtkunstwerk* on this level, as they continued their self-curation. But to fully comprehend Kraftwerk's *Gesamtkunstwerk*, we need to return to their formative years in Düsseldorf and cast a closer eye on the influence of the artistic scene in the Rhine-Ruhr area (and Germany in general) on the band. Sorry: the group of artists.

Joseph Beuys and the Extended Definition of Art

Joseph Beuys was born in Krefeld, a town near Düsseldorf – as was Ralf Hütter, twenty-five years later. Of all the artists who shaped the Düsseldorf art scene, such as Gerhard Richter, Anselm Kiefer and Sigmar Polke, Beuys was surely the most prominent, not least because of his personal charisma. Beuys, who was a frequent visitor at the villa of Florian Schneider's family, taught at the Academy of Art from 1961 until his controversial dismissal in 1972. Due to his many provocative public performances and happenings, he was well known beyond the confines of the art academy.

Beuys's major contribution to the development of modern art was his extended definition of art, which claimed that 'everyone can be an artist'. Though this slogan is often understood in a trivial sense, its philosophical, social and aesthetic implications reach much deeper. Beuys's aesthetic thinking evolves around his idea of the 'social sculpture'. Its key notion is the idea that art can act as a healing force for a sick society. Regarding society as a whole as the foremost 'material' of the artist, Beuys sees it as the artist's duty to produce art that 'moulds' society through aesthetics. Art is allocated the role of creating a beautiful 'sculpture' out of an ugly reality of social tensions and the detrimental effects of capitalism.

Beuys's 'extended' understanding of the term 'sculpture' evidently bears a distinct resemblance to Kraftwerk's robot aesthetics. This holds particularly true for the idea of creating life-like dummy replicas of each band member, thus attempting to fashion them into sculptures of sorts. A closely related example within the world of art are Gilbert & George's 'living sculpture' shows, particularly their *Singing Sculpture* performances, in which they appeared coated in metallic make-up, standing generally still like dummies, making only sparse movements, while singing the music-hall classic 'Underneath the Arches' by Bud Flanagan and Chesney Allen. These performances would last for a total of eight hours (with short breaks). Konrad Fischer arranged for the London artists to appear at the Kunsthalle in Düsseldorf in 1970.

'We saw *The Singing Sculpture* of Gilbert & George in Düsseldorf, of course,' Hütter conceded in 2006, though he added, misleadingly: 'It was not particularly influential on us.'[12] Once again, Hütter was aiming to obscure any evident inspiration, trying to make the (early) Kraftwerk 'formula' appear more original than it actually was in order to over-emphasize their singularity. But there can be little doubt: the way in which Gilbert & George reworked a very British musical tradition into maverick art was very similar to the way in which Hütter and Schneider as *Ralf and Florian* – Mr Kling and Mr Klang – would develop a new type of music, connected with specific aspects of German cultural history.

Another reference point for Kraftwerk was the industrial photography of conceptual-artist couple Hilla and Bernd Becher. They are best known for their extensive series of photographic images of functional buildings, machines and industrial structures. Belonging to what became known as the 'Düsseldorf school' of photography, they began in the late fifties to document disappearing industrial architecture: cooling towers, gas tanks, oil refineries, blast furnaces and coal bunkers, and so on.

Related motifs were arranged in a grid to create what they called 'typologies' of the industrial tradition in the Rhein-Ruhr heartland of German industrialization. Among the motifs photographed, of course, were power stations, *Kraftwerke* in German – which might have been a possible source for the choice of band name.

The architectural remnants of a bygone age were deemed by the Bechers to be, according to their book, published in Düsseldorf in 1970, *Anonyme*

Skulpturen (*Anonymous Sculptures*). The couple's art is based on the idea that photography – itself a technical medium – can be employed to elevate the relics of industrial culture to the status of art. As such, they were following a path similar to Kraftwerk, who aimed to elevate industrial noise into art by the technological means of music machines.

Hütter and Schneider were verifiably aware of the work of the Bechers, as they included a large-format photograph of a free-standing electrical transformer on the fold-up inner sleeve of the first *Kraftwerk* album in 1970. The relationship of the transformer to the emerging conceptual aesthetics of the band hardly needs to be elucidated: electricity is what drives modern technology, and the concept of the transformation of the everyday into art is what largely defined the musical concept of Kraftwerk.

But apart from such tentative links to the conceptual ideas that floated around in the Düsseldorf art scene of the day, there also exists a very direct link from Beuys to Kraftwerk: Emil Schult, the unofficial fifth member of Kraftwerk.

The Role of Emil Schult

As Karl Bartos recalls: 'When I joined up with Kraftwerk in 1975, I found an already existing visual identity. Looking at the record covers, a proximity to the visual arts was evident. Also, the stage design resembled an audiovisual installation. Everything was dipped into neon light and looked extremely artificial.'[13]

Largely responsible for this resemblance to artistic strategies was none other than former Beuys student Emil Schult: 'My input with the band was always part of a larger artistic dialogue, which included visual ideas that were developed together. It wasn't just give and take; it was also about developing things conceptually in parallel processes.'[14]

It was Florian Schneider who introduced Emil Schult to Kraftwerk. Around 1973, he went to see a fellow Düsseldorf band whose violin player turned out to be Schult. He had constructed an electronic violin, something that Schneider himself was interested in building, so he invited Schult over to the Kling Klang studio. For a brief time, Düsseldorf-born Schult became a member of the Kraftwerk line-up. Allegedly, he once played the guitar while roller-skating across the stage. However, it soon turned out that he would be far more useful as the band's source of ideas, conceptualist, artistic contributor and, importantly, in interfacing with the local art scene and the world of art in general.

Often overlooked and underestimated, Schult's

contribution to the Kraftwerk *Gesamtkunstwerk* reaches far beyond their iconic cover illustrations. From *Ralf and Florian* onwards, his influence on the visual identity of Kraftwerk is clearly discernible. For one, the neon signs displaying the two names on the back-cover image were made on his recommendation. The idea behind them was to reflect the many examples of neon advertisements in the area around the Kling Klang studio. These, of course, later also inspired the beautiful 'Neon Lights'. The 'Ralf' and 'Florian' signs would also feature on stage when Hütter and Schneider appeared as a duo; later, signs reading 'Karl' and 'Wolfgang' were duly added.

It was also Schult's idea to complement the music on *Ralf and Florian* with his 'musicomics'. These were pop-art-influenced cartoons and drawings showing portraits of (mostly female) members of their immediate circle – girlfriends, sisters, mothers, even a woman from a local record shop. Schult claimed that 'if you know the group, you can really see what a mix of ideas and input it is, visually speaking'.[15] Florian Schneider agreed: 'When I met Emil and when he showed his comics to me, I thought that they looked like our music.'[16]

Schult's cartoons (and the few sketches Schneider contributed) were an expression of the Warhol-inspired notion of making art from the everyday, both in terms of music and pop-art-styled cartoons. Kraftwerk would return to the idea of using drawings when designing the inner sleeve of *Trans-Europe Express*. It showed little cartoons which encapsulated each track on the album visually, this time drawn in a style that was less childlike and related more directly to the music.

It was under Schult's guidance that Kraftwerk began to deliberately pursue the idea of a broader artistic concept that would incorporate a variety of activities, following the model of Warhol's Factory but also the Wagnerian notion of a *Gesamtkunstwerk*. In addition to music, these activities would comprise their album-sleeve designs and the films they made to use as projections during concerts, the development of new equipment, the establishment and management of the Kling Klang Verlag to publish Kraftwerk's output, the external representation of the Kling Klang activities through interviews, and so on. 'We don't think of ourselves as musicians,' Hütter pointed out provocatively, 'but rather as people who create out of different media or ways of expressing yourself, whether it is painting, poetry, music or even film. The idea is to communicate to people.'[17]

In an interview with Pascal Bussy, Schult confirmed that his role had been that of a guru or muse for the group: 'I was always there, people would give me their ideas and I would interpret them. I wouldn't say that my talent was especially musical, but you know, I had an influence on everything, that's how it is, when you are in a group you have influence on everything.'[18]

From early on, Kraftwerk understood that such clips would greatly help to forge their visual identity. They enlisted the services of cameraman Günter Fröhling, who was skilfully able to replicate the look and feel of twenties Weimar cinema, which is what Hütter and Schneider wanted. In January 1976, Fröhling started shooting for the 'Radio-activity' clip at the Kling Klang studio; the video was essentially the documentation of a live performance but embellished with visually impressive sequences such as two hands making mechanical movements.[19]

The Kraftwerk videos overseen by Schult connected German Expressionist cinema with the experimental short films Warhol had produced since the sixties and the emerging video art pioneered by Nam June Paik, as well as the films shown during Fluxus performances. It is remarkable that Kraftwerk placed such great importance on the conversion of sound and vision by means of these clips, given that there was no existing music television as such in the pre-MTV age. Once more, Hütter and Schneider had sensed what was to come and were ahead of their time.

Schult didn't just work at the Kling Klang studio; he was also often around during tours. His duty was to sort out unexpected problems, acting in the role of an artistic tour manager, or, as the band decided to baptize him, as Kraftwerk's 'vibrations manager'. But with Kraftwerk's production and release activities slowing down during the eighties, Schult's involvement diminished. In 1982, he moved to the Bahamas, essentially cutting off his working relationship with the band; he remained in the Caribbean until the mid-nineties.

For Kraftwerk, the focus was now firmly on digitalization and cycling, requiring little input in terms of novel design ideas. Even so, Schult supplied an unsolicited draft of some cover artwork for *The Mix*, a sort of collage of previous album covers, which was ultimately rejected by Hütter and Schneider. Similarly, for *Electric Café* they opted to work with Rebecca Allan's computer-generated graphics for both the promotional video and the cover design (though Schult received a credit for the artwork too).

Once the work on the digitalization had been completed, efforts shifted to other concerns. Oddly enough, Kraftwerk did embark on, and finish, a new studio album. Or to be more precise, some original songs were added to the existing corpus of cycling-related songs. The true degree to which the *Tour de France Soundtracks* album from 2003 consists of genuinely new 'music data' is difficult, if not impossible, to ascertain.

In any case, the *Expo2000* EP, released in December 1999, definitely featured a new song, developed out of the jingle commissioned for the Hanover world fair in 2000. But this flurry of recording activity around the turn of the millennium was, sadly, only a one-off. A detour to the recording studio, if you like. Once more, the focus soon shifted back to the revision of the existing music, this time in terms of digital remastering.

Along with this sonic improvement of the eight albums for the *Catalogue* box set came a parallel visual effort – an update of their artwork. To help with this, Emil Schult was enlisted to help again. Along with two other designers, Schult worked on the transformation of the images he had helped to create into three-dimensional visuals for the stage shows. His most notable success is the film that now accompanies 'Autobahn', which brings his iconic painting truly alive by taking the onlooker on a journey along the motorway: a genuine musical painting.

Updated Designs of *The Catalogue*: Simplification and Monochrome

The second decade of the twenty-first century saw some important developments in the history of Kraftwerk. For one, the Kling Klang studio moved to an undisclosed location outside Düsseldorf. However, Lise-Meitner-Strasse in Meerbusch, a small town between Düsseldorf and Krefeld, is given as the business address of Kraftwerk. One can therefore assume that the new studio must also be located at this address, or at least nearby. Being a faceless business park, however, the area does not lend itself to becoming a place of pilgrimage, as the old Kling Klang studio had.

This relocation, most likely a decision taken by Hütter alone, more or less coincided with the release of the *Catalogue* collection in November 2009, a crucial one in their discography. *The Catalogue* marked the thirty-fifth anniversary of the release of *Autobahn* (November 1974). However, the box set was already finished in 2004, in time for its thirtieth anniversary. Originally entitled *The Catalogue – 12345678*, there exist a few, now ultra-rare, promo copies of the box. The reason it took another five years until it finally surfaced is, of course, unknown.[20]

There are some minor mixing differences between the 2004 and the 2009 versions of *The Catalogue*, which do not warrant much attention, other than by true Kraftwerk nerds. Small adjustments were made to the album titles – *Tour de France* lost the word 'Soundtracks' and, crucially, the original title, *Techno Pop*, was restored to *Electric Cafe*. In addition, 'The Telephone Call' – the only Kraftwerk track written and sung by Karl Bartos – was replaced by the shorter, single version, and the remix 'House Phone' added. While the latter is a great track worthy of elevation from its previous status as the B-side to a single, this in itself cannot conceal the likelihood that the change was motivated by the desire to minimize Bartos's contribution to the album as much as possible without actually dropping the track.

The hallmark of *The Catalogue* was its improved sound quality. The new Kling Klang Digital Masters naturally sounded better than the original analogue tapes, yet apart from the changes detailed above all eight key studio albums had essentially remained the same. The artwork, however, was in some cases altered beyond all recognition. Evidently, the visual aspects of the *Gesamtkunstwerk* took on greater importance once Kraftwerk's musical work was finally done in 2003 with the release of *Tour de France*, probably their final studio album.

Now, heralded by *The Catalogue*, it was back to their roots in the art scene that had originally given birth to the band. The overarching tendency to streamline the visual appearance of the eight albums resulted in major design changes to the first three records: *Autobahn* now featured the internationally recognized traffic sign, *Radio-Activity* saw the Nazi radio set replaced by the trefoil warning symbol for radiation, and *Trans-Europe Express* similarly did away with the nostalgic band portraits in favour of a highly stylized rendering of the Trans Europ Express.

Overall, the design revamp favoured abstract symbols over figurative depictions, semiotics over realism, while at the same time expounding the visual power of the elementary colours blue (*Autobahn*), yellow and red (*Radio-Activity*) and black and white (*Trans-Europe Express*). This colour code could now become part of a visual dialogue with the other album covers: the red of *The Man-Machine*, the yellow of *Computer World*, the black of *Techno Pop* and the blue/white/red/black combination of *Tour de France*.

Such minimalism made the *Gesamtkunstwerk* more visually coherent and abstract, not least due to the exorcism of all band photos. Only the computer-generated polygon faces on the re-christened *Techno Pop* remind listeners today of the fact that four human musicians (rather than anonymous music workers) recorded these albums.

The deliberate oversimplification of the visual language of the cover artwork, however, was balanced by the LP-sized booklets that accompanied the digital remasters. These reproduced lost artwork, obscure single designs, old inner-sleeve designs, stills from videos and even the odd previously unseen image. The booklet to *The Man-Machine*, for instance, contains various rarely seen double-page images of the robots in their trademark outfit of red shirt, black tie and grey trousers. The large size of these photographs makes them look particularly striking. Buyers of the *Catalogue* box set could not help but notice that the visual aspect had now become as important as sound to Kraftwerk, and, beyond this, that the albums were now more clearly related to each other as part of the same *Gesamtkunstwerk*.

The *Catalogue*-Complex

The Catalogue was first presented live at the Kraftwerk residence at the Museum of Modern Art in April 2012. Billed as a retrospective – up until this time a term usually reserved for works of art only – it announced a new chapter in the performance history of the band. However, it wasn't the first time that the art project Kraftwerk had become the subject of a museum exhibition.

From then on, Kraftwerk time and again entered a realm commonly associated with art, not pop music: museums, galleries and exhibition spaces, thus completing the circle that began with their early appearances at art galleries. Once more, the band was groundbreaking in this move: it would be another year before museums (or their curators) decided that pop music was an area of art worth exhibiting. (Later retrospectives include the great exhibition of David Bowie memorabilia at the Victoria & Albert Museum in London in 2013 and the Björk exhibition at the New York Museum of Modern Art in 2015.)

A few minor contributions to exhibitions aside, the first time Kraftwerk played a prominent part in an art show occurred in 1999/2000. Coinciding with the release of the *Expo2000* EP, the four robot dummies, featuring the newly updated faces of Hütter and Schneider, were shown at an exhibition of the Haus der Geschichte (House of History) in Bonn. In a way, sending their dummies to exhibitions chimed with the song lyrics to 'Showroom Dummies' (1977), where Kraftwerk proudly declare (though the English translation is somewhat unfortunate): 'We are standing here/Exposing ourselves/We are show-room dummies'.

In early 2002, the dummies featured in an exhibition entitled *Ex Machina – Eine Geschichte des Roboters von 1950 bis heute* (*A History of the Robot from 1950 to the Present*) at the Cologne Museum of Applied Art; in the autumn of the same year, they were shown at the Cité de la Musique in Paris on the occasion of Kraftwerk's concerts in the French capital.

A considerable step forward in the recognition of Kraftwerk by the art scene was their invitation by the Lenbachhaus museum in Munich to show their visuals at the underground Kunstbau exhibition space between October and November 2011. Strictly speaking, this exhibition comprised multichannel 3D video installations of key 'musical paintings'.

Standing alone, they now warranted the same attention as installations by recognized video artists. Since their Munich debut, Kraftwerk's 3D installations were repeatedly shown, for instance at the MoMA concerts in New York and Stockholm. The status of Kraftwerk as a *Gesamtkunstwerk* was further confirmed when the internationally successful gallery Sprüth Magers announced that they now represented the band.

As it happened, Ralf Hütter had known

co-director Monika Sprüth since 1968; she, too, had studied architecture at Aachen University and the two had shared a house. In a way, it felt as if Kraftwerk had finally arrived: drawing manifold inspirations for their gradual development from the world of art, they were now fully recognized as an art project and exhibited in a museum context.

The Munich exhibition in 2011 also provided the occasion for three concerts at the Alte Kongresshalle, unveiling their full 3D shows for the first time. Like any other major exhibition, it was accompanied by a catalogue, simply called *Kraftwerk 3-D*. It featured iconic stills from the visuals transformed by traditional stereoscopic technique to create 3D-effects through the colour anaglyphic method, popular in seventies books of optical illusions for children. Reviewing the book, renowned photographer and sculptor Thomas Demand hailed Kraftwerk for their dedication to their key themes: 'The real progress in Kraftwerk's body of work lies in their unwavering focus. [. . .] True mastery comes from working with a given motif over years and years, if not decades.'

With regard to the images in the book, he observed:

In 3D reproduction, the book's most intriguing images are those that move away from a certain photo-realism. It sounds paradoxical, but the more graphic and two-dimensional the images are, the more effective they become in 3D – not only on the page, but also live. [. . .] Even though the book is more like a roadmap than a real landscape, it remains an important documentation of the band's reclamation of their cutting-edge status and role as musical and visual pioneers. This is a picture book in its purest form, and the particular charm of *Kraftwerk 3-D* lies in its visual details: its complete lack of text, intentionally clumsy 3D renderings and pale colouring.[21]

Kraftwerk 3-D wasn't the first book by Kraftwerk. The limited-edition version of *Minimum-Maximum* came in a box designed to resemble a laptop; apart from the enclosed double CD and double DVD sets, it also contained a book featuring a computer keyboard on its cover. The hardcover volume, too, contained stills from the live visuals, but also concert photos, as well as images showing the robots in various poses. These photographs were taken by Peter Boettcher, who has acted as exclusive photographer to Kraftwerk for a number of years.

On his website, Boettcher describes his artistic approach as follows: 'Boettcher's portraits of the robots and his photographs of the group's stage performances during concerts around the world capture the essence of the Kraftwerk universe. Through the reduced forms and colours, the graphical severity of the photos, and the consistent use of the central perspective for concert photos, Peter Boettcher captures Kraftwerk's image world in a congenial manner.'[22] After allowing for the inevitable self-advertising, this blurb still provides a fair characterization of his photographic reflection of Kraftwerk's aesthetics.

Following various exhibitions that accompanied *The Catalogue – 12345678* retrospectives, Boettcher's work of defining Kraftwerk's visual identity in the medium of photography was documented in the book *Kraftwerk Roboter*, published in 2013. His evocative images, taken between 1991 and 2009, show the robot dummies in various contexts. Particularly impressive are the shots taken in the Kling Klang studio for *The Mix*, for example showing the robots operating the studio machinery bathed in cool blue light.

The eerie series of close-up head shots and the image depicting them positioned in front of their travel containers reveal the dummies in ways one would not normally encounter them. The volume concludes with a photograph that creates a lasting impact: 'Konzentration' from 2009 depicts the face of the dummy representing Hütter with closed eyes against a largely black background; it uncannily oscillates between death mask and a very life-like impression of a robot in the very human state of concentration.

The graphic design of this book was the work of Johann Zambryski, who had gained a name for himself as an album-cover designer for a number of successful German bands. He had also assisted Kraftwerk with the revision of the cover artwork for the *Catalogue* box set (through which the artistic signature of Emil Schult became largely eradicated from the Kraftwerk visual cosmos). It is hence only fair to say that the team of Zambryski and Boettcher have now largely (though not entirely) replaced the earlier crucial collaborators Emil Schult and Günter Fröhling. It is the job of these two new collaborators to ensure that Kraftwerk's visual identity remains coherently abstract and stringent.

In retrospect, it became clear that the minimalist design of the front of the *Catalogue* box set introduced a new formal language in regard to their graphic design. Band name and title were given in a nostalgic low-resolution, pixellated bitmap typography reminiscent of the dawn of our computer world. It is important to note now that this deliberate retro typography would return on all successive releases and official merchandise – the two books mentioned, T-shirts and posters, but also on the website, on concert tickets, on the 3D glasses handed out at live shows, and so on.

The *Catalogue* design also introduced the minimalist Kraftwerk avatar showing the four band members as abstracted figures composed of pixels in an eight-by-twelve grid. Through its manifold recurrence across all things Kraftwerk, the schematic design now constitutes their logo. As a result of this ubiquity, the pictogram forms an organic part of the semiotic cosmos of Kraftwerk, along with the motorway sign or the radiation-warning symbol. The correspondence between the design of musical releases, books and other paraphernalia, as well as the obvious connection to *The Catalogue – 12345678* concert series, allows us to categorize their activities since 2009 under the term '*Catalogue*-complex'.

A vital part of this complex is their official website, www.kraftwerk.com, launched in December 1996. From the beginning, care was taken not to emulate the sophisticated Web design standard that characterized comparable websites. Kraftwerk, as always, wanted to be different. The main component deliberately missing from the website is any form of virtual contact with their fan base – no mailing list, no discussion forum, no competitions to win signed copies or backstage passes allowing fans to hang out with the boys after a show.

Nor is there any official history of the band, as found on almost all other band websites. That is of course part of their artistic strategy of myth-making. Instead, the website currently features a series of photographs in anti-chronological order, covering key moments in the live history of the last ten years. There are only two things it shares with a standard band website: firstly, the link to mail-order merchandise, the Kling Klang Konsum Prod-ukt shop; secondly, the concert section, listing gigs played from 2002 to the present and, more crucially, announcing forthcoming shows.

The scarcity of information provided, as well as the lack of opportunities to interact with the band via an official fan club or similar, is fully in line with Kraftwerk's principle of minimalism and privacy. But it also reflects Ralf Hütter's reservations about the internet as a communication tool and his known scorn for social media: 'I am not a fan of the internet. I think it is overrated. Intelligent information is still intelligent information and an overflow of nonsense does not really help. In German, it's called *Daten-müll*: data rubbish.'[23]

What will strike visitors to the website who are unfamiliar with the Kraftwerk aesthetic as surprisingly retro and outdated is the decision to align the purposefully simple Web design with the design guidelines of the *Catalogue*-complex. As befits a true *Gesamtkunstwerk*, the Kraftwerk œuvre now comprises a truly postmodern, multimedia conglomeration of Web design, graphic design, typography, photography and digital media on the one hand, and visuals, music, lyrics and stage-performance practice on the other. Having long left behind the context of mere pop music, they now operate in an arena that lies somewhere between the music industry and the art world.

3–D *The Catalogue*: Increased Minimalism

In May 2017 Kraftwerk issued the second incarnation of the *Catalogue* box set: a comprehensive document of their live shows during the second decade of the twenty-first century. With live recordings in pristine sound quality taken from regular concerts and *The Catalogue – 12345678* shows since 2013, *3-D The Catalogue* expands the visual component of Kraftwerk live even further. On Blu-ray and DVD, the collected visuals document the renewed energy with which Kraftwerk pushed the development of their audiovisual project.

The glowing advertisements filmed by Günter Fröhling in 1978 in night-time Düsseldorf still float across the screen during 'Neon Lights', creating a truly nostalgic, retro-futurist feel: audiences will see well-known German brand logos like Universum, Klosterfrau, UFA, Deutsche Bank and Mercedes-Benz, but also the neon sign attracting male customers to the seedy bars opposite the Kling Klang studio and the slogan of a well-known city-centre optician – *Gut sehen, besser hören* (See more, hear better) – which of course gains an entirely new meaning within the context of the forty-channel, 3D audiovisual spectacle that is a Kraftwerk concert today.

3-D The Catalogue represents the next – probably final – evolution of the artwork of Kraftwerk's impressive catalogue of albums. The tendency towards design minimalism was taken even further. The bitmap typography and the abstract pixel group representing the band of course remained. However, instead of neutral white as the background colour of the 2009 *Catalogue* version, the 2017 *3-D The Catalogue* was colour-coded an intense red.

Similarly, the eight albums contained in the box were now stripped of all individual artwork, leaving just numbers (from 1 to 8) and monochrome colours (based on the design revisions of *The Catalogue*), for example, blue for *Autobahn*, yellow for *Radio-Activity* and black for *Trans-Europe Express*. This also explained the colour choice for the box itself, as only one album was colour-coded red: it is, of course, *The Man-Machine*. It could not have been any clearer that Kraftwerk consider *3-D The Catalogue* to be the quintessence of the man-machine concept – a document of the Kraftwerk aesthetic in its purest manifestation.

In line with the design principles introduced for the *Catalogue*-complex, a small version of the pixel pictogram representing the band now uniformly adorns each album, making it somewhat difficult for the uninitiated listener to identify them. What this radical step of abolishing individual artwork suggests is that Kraftwerk's *Gesamtkunstwerk* is intended to be perceived as one body of albums, consisting of different components or colour facets but forming one great whole.

This implies an invitation to dissolve the boundaries between the individual albums. Like a rainbow, the beauty arises from the symphony of the various colours. The ideal scenario, it seems, would therefore be to listen to and look at *3-D The Catalogue* as simply one long flow of music and image.

How Kraftwerk can build on *3-D The Catalogue* remains to be seen. It is difficult to imagine that the minimalist thrust could be continued now that the stage of monochrome design has been reached. Maybe the artistic idea is to look beyond the visible. Regarding the interplay between sound and vision, Ralf Hütter once explained that 'Kraftwerk songs are meant to open people's eyes to a new electronic future; they are acoustic impulses that seek to induce a strong visual experience within the listener.'[24] A futuristic sense of synaesthesia may well be the ultimate goal of Kraftwerk.

7. 'MUSIC NON STOP': KRAFTWERK'S LEGACY

Peter Boettcher

Robots in front of Detroit State Theater in June 1998.

What is Kraftwerk's legacy? Were they as (or even more) important than The Beatles in the development of pop music? Could, for example, techno have emerged from inner-city areas of Detroit without them? And to what extent did their early decision to remain fiercely independent, running their own label and, more significantly, their own studio, set a model for other bands and producers? How did the overarching concept of the man-machine influence later (male and female) artists in the realm of electronic music? And are Kraftwerk not just a man-machine but also a myth-machine?

The most notable legacy of the band is perhaps its conceptual engagement with electronic music, particularly the way in which Kraftwerk pioneered the interaction between (hu)man and machine. That is to say: the true legacy of Kraftwerk cannot merely be heard in electronic music everywhere, it can also often be seen in the way electronic music and the visual arts have converged, as well as in how electronic-music artists choose to present themselves and their music on stage.

Electronic Pop Music as Concept Art

What Kraftwerk began to do as early as the release of *Ralf and Florian* (1973), more than any comparable band, was to think conceptually and place the concept before the music. Starting with *Autobahn*, Kraftwerk released only concept albums from 1974 onwards. But their motivation to do so differed from that of the prog-rock bands that also released over-wrought concept albums during the seventies, such as *The Lamb Lies Down on Broadway* (1974) by British art-rockers Genesis.

Kraftwerk were trying to turn *themselves* into a concept, and it was their determination to work primarily with concepts (such as retro-futurism, minimalism, everyday themes or indeed their very own invention, *industrielle Volksmusik*) that changed the way in which pop music could be conceived. They saw their work as an expression of the artistic revolution that was the conceptual-art movement, which gained particular traction with the Fluxus movement. It is perhaps no coincidence that the foundation of Kraftwerk in 1970 coincided with the first dedicated exhibition of conceptual art (*Conceptual Art and Conceptual Aspects* at the New York Cultural Center).

Kraftwerk very much aimed to 'translate' what

was happening in the art scene into the medium of pop music. Here is one of Hütter's odd trademark statements, designed to create a unique identity for the band within the framework of pop music: 'We are not musicians, we are rather scientists,' he announced. 'Kraftwerk is not chords and numbers, but rather a realistic concept to transpose ideas to their maximum. Ideas come to us as we are working.'[1] With the group itself defined primarily as a concept, it is little surprise that Kraftwerk opted for the format of the concept album as their main form of artistic output.

However, Kraftwerk's conceptual-art approach not only applied to their albums but also to how they styled and presented themselves in public. After all, Hütter and Schneider are notoriously private. 'The whole ego aspect of music is boring,' Hütter explained. 'It doesn't interest us.'[2] This resulted in the conceptual decision to present Kraftwerk as a uniform, anonymous group of 'music workers'. The collective group identity is far more important than that of the individuals involved.

As Karl Bartos remembers: 'The initial image really came from Ralf. He wanted to make it clear that Kraftwerk was different from any other pop or rock group and he wanted this image of a string ensemble.'[3] Suit and tie, accessorized to comic effect with a brooch in the shape of an oversized treble clef, subverted the serious image. Hütter and Schneider created a band persona decidedly at odds with the standard styling of a pop-music group (jeans paired with boots and leather jackets). Like all uniforms, it was also a disguise behind which they could hide.

In sharp contrast to most rock stars, Hütter and Schneider didn't want, as the lyrics to 'Hall of Mirrors' (1977) state, to 'live their life in the looking glass' of media scrutiny. This complex song about the loss and recovery of identity references, among other things, the myth of Narcissus, but it is also a reflection on pop stardom. The 'greatest star' repeatedly mentioned can be none other than David Bowie during his drug-fuelled Los Angeles period. Unlike him, Kraftwerk shied away from being an object of public interest, seeing the fate of Bowie as a cautionary tale: 'The artist is living in the mirror/ With the echoes of himself/Even the greatest stars/ Change themselves in the looking glass'.

And it is for that reason, too, that they began to employ their famous robot dummy *doppelgängers* as an elegant way to distance their personal lives from the enquiries of journalists. It also afforded an opportunity to escape the tiresome duty of posing for publicity photographs. The last official press photograph taken of the band was the group portrait for *The Man-Machine* in 1978, which already showed them in quite a dehumanized manner, resembling robots. From *Computer World* (1981) onwards, Kraftwerk replaced the humans with their robot doubles.

Though it was still recognizably Ralf Hütter, Karl Bartos, Wolfgang Flür and Florian Schneider who featured on the cover of *The Man-Machine*, in conceptual terms the robot dummies projected the group's corporate identity: Kraftwerk. This modus operandi had several advantages: it thwarted the curiosity and personal attentions of fans; it built a wall of mystique around the group; and it, eventually, made it easy to replace individual musicians – even one of the founding members. Why? Because Kraftwerk is more than the sum of its parts, existing as a concept (primarily conceived, developed from the beginning and now solely maintained by Ralf Hütter).

One crucial idea stressed time and time again is the concept of *Alltagsmusik* (everyday music): 'The world around us is a complete orchestra to us,' Hütter explained. 'The noises from cars, coffee machines, and vacuum cleaners, we can use for our music. That is like a film. We are the scriptwriters, who with their ears pick up everything and bring in new pictures. I don't listen to music from other people any more. At home, I turn on no music. I don't need that. I can think my music.'[4] Such statements, and there are many of this ilk, betray the purposeful effort to construct Kraftwerk's unique image.

As he'd said ten years earlier: 'We like to portray the things we do on a day-to-day basis in our music [. . .] everyday technology, such as cars, trains and other human-controlled machines.'[5] The avant-garde aspiration to elevate the trivial and previously overlooked into art plainly provides the background to the concept of everyday music. 'Writers and poets play with words and phrases, painters with colours and angles of view, and Kraftwerk play with noises,'[6] runs another of Hütter's declarations of artistic intent.

In many cases, the sounds and noises on Kraftwerk records are what academics call indexical: they refer directly to everyday sources such as the horn of a car, the heavy breathing of a human being, the dialling noise of an outdated analogue telephone set, the whirring of a bicycle chain or, indeed, the industrial noise of hitting metal on metal. As indexical noises, they correspond to the musical onomatopoeia of earlier classical music.

Just think, for instance, of the gurgling sounds of the Vlatava (Moldau) river re-created in Bedřich Smetana's 'symphonic poem', first performed in 1875. Similarly, sounds of nature are imitated in Ludwig van Beethoven's sixth symphony, the

Pastorale, while Gustav Mahler reproduced the sounds of cow bells in his work. The decisive difference is that Kraftwerk play the music truly befitting the (post-)industrial age of the twentieth century and the digital age of the twenty-first.

Other statements habitually issued by Hütter on Kraftwerk's artistic goals and musical ambition state their intention to 'bring man and machine together in a friendly partnership of musical creation' and declare that 'we are neither artists nor musicians. We are workers.'[7] Indeed, the artistic notion of the man-machine and the austere conception of themselves as workers represent the most important aspects of Kraftwerk's musical-conceptual art.

Man, Machine, Minimalism

Another defining characteristic of Kraftwerk's art is the principle of minimalism in music, adapted from the minimalist movement in American art of the early sixties. With Kraftwerk, there is an intellectual process at work which precedes the musical process. It also governs other aspects of production, such as the artwork, stage design, concert posters and much more, always aiming to achieve a sense of clarity, soberness and objectivity through minimalism.

Hütter attributed the predominance of this

principle to their use of machines: 'Our music is rather minimalist. [. . .] With our musical machines, there is no question of playing them with a kind of virtuosity, there is all the virtuosity we need in the machines, so we concentrated our work towards a very direct minimalism.'[8] Minimalist principles in pop music require a rejection of the notion of authenticity. The concept of authenticity is part and parcel of rock and folk music – take Billy Bragg, for example: his fans expect him to believe in what he sings and see his songs as a truthful reflection of English working-class experience.

Kraftwerk, however, did not subscribe to such an approach. Their emphasis, on the contrary, was on the non-authentic, the impersonal, the serial – principles that are more akin to the nature of electronic music and a strict adherence to artistic concepts. Or in other words: Kraftwerk has none of the heat of rock'n'roll but instead pioneered a different model of pop music, the coldness and the cool stemming from the use of machines.

With this approach, they set the blueprint for all later bands and musicians working in the area of electronic music. Just think of the robotic movements of Gary Numan, whose biggest hit was 1979's 'Cars' (a rip-off of 'Autobahn', of course). His hit 'Are "Friends" Electric?' betrays even more blatantly the debt he owes to the Kraftwerk formula to replace humans with robots.

Another instructive example is provided by electronica wizard Aphex Twin, which is just one of dozens of monikers behind which erratic genius Richard D. James hides to release widely differing music with a totally unpredictable irregularity – in the same way in which Kraftwerk hide artistically behind the anonymity provided by their man-machine concept and are also very difficult to predict in their upcoming moves, not to mention their release schedule.

The *Gesamtkunstwerk* of Kraftwerk

Whether Kraftwerk or The Beatles were more influential has long been a bone of contention among journalists and fans. To engage with this question is, of course, pointless. What can be safely stated, however, is that Kraftwerk accomplished the biggest revolution in popular music since The Beatles. They changed the course of modern music by pioneering the concept of an electronic pop music. Or as Neil Straus argued: 'What The Beatles are to rock music, Kraftwerk is to electronic dance music.'[9]

The distinctive feature differentiating Kraftwerk from other pivotal bands is that their artistic influence extends beyond the realm of music. Exhibiting their 3D visuals in museums and galleries, Kraftwerk has inspired, among many others, the graphic designers Neville Brody and Peter Saville (of seminal Manchester label Factory Records). 'I am very influenced by Kraftwerk,' Saville confessed. 'They shaped my understanding of the possibilities of contemporary music, and that shapes my understanding of the visual language that can be associated with it. [. . .] The culture of Factory is highly informed by Kraftwerk: and it's Factory that pretty much defines Manchester culturally in the late 20th century.'[10]

Naturally, the complete artistic package that is Kraftwerk proved a guiding force for artists born in Germany. In the fine arts, the internationally successful German artists Thomas Demand and Andreas Gursky owe a self-confessed debt to the band: their photographic art was hugely inspired by the cover images of the Kraftwerk releases they bought as teenagers or young adults. German director Rainer Werner Fassbinder, too, was hugely influenced by Kraftwerk, featuring their music on some of the soundtracks to his films. 'On set, his team of actors would at times be forced to listen to either "Autobahn" or "Radioactivity", setting the mood for the various film scenes, until they could no longer endure it.'[11]

The Kraftwerk œuvre has left its traces in German literature, too, for instance in the experimental prose texts of German avant-garde writer Andreas Neumeister, or the brilliant novel *Pale Blue* (*Hellblau*) (2001) by Thomas Meinecke. His book contains fascinating sections in which the protagonists debate the remixes which members of the Detroit Underground Resistance collective have made of Kraftwerk's 'Expo2000' track.

But what is it that made Kraftwerk's output so important for artists across all these disciplines? It exerted such a strong influence across a range of different art forms because their artistic creations operate on various levels, including but not limited to the musical. Hütter and Schneider, as already discussed, found their most immediate inspiration to pursue such a bold artistic undertaking from the multimedia activities of Andy Warhol. The Factory, his studio space in New York, was replete with painters, writers, designers and idle starlets, surrounding and supplementing Warhol's activities as an artist and film-maker. It was a collective effort, under Warhol's curatorship, albeit one which was presented to the wider world as Warhol's singular vision.

Similarly, Kraftwerk has to be understood as greater than the sum of its parts; Barr spells this out appositely: 'Hütter's and Schneider's attitude is to treat everything they do as Kraftwerk – record releases, touring, sleeve design, image, even the rare interviews they grant – as part of the same piece. The total work of art in this case *is* Kraftwerk.'[12] Hütter himself says on the matter:

Kraftwerk is really a multimedia concept. Not just music. But we compose words and images, and that's in a way what's related to the atmosphere in the late Sixties in Düsseldorf when I started with my partner Florian in '68, and later in the 1970s when we started the Kling Klang studio with just a tape recorder. But coming from there, it's a different approach than coming from a musical tradition. We come from nowhere.[13]

This last sentence can safely be classified as yet another attempt to mythologize Kraftwerk. Over the course of the decades, Ralf Hütter has spent a considerable amount of energy covering Kraftwerk's tracks, probably knowing full well that this mystique greatly adds to the appeal of the band. Kraftwerk are not just a man-machine, they are also a myth-machine.

Inside the Kling Klang Studio: Kraftwerk and Myth-making

Kraftwerk operate according to their own rules. These include a considerable degree of myth-mongering, as we have already seen from their interview statements. Hütter and Schneider also instigated an increasingly strict policy of refusing to discuss the workings of the Kling Klang studio.

Instead, they fed the interested public stories like the following tale of the accidental 'discovery' of the instrumental 'Franz Schubert' on *Trans-Europe Express*: 'I was switching on the sequencing machines and it was playing,' Hütter recalled.

> It was something else we'd been setting up before, something much speedier, the machines just happened to be tuned at that thing the next day and I played it. I changed the octaves and I thought it was Schubert playing, like he's saying hello because he is the master of German melodies. So it's like Schubert just came in for a few minutes and said hello to the machine spirit.[14]

So, despite discouraging unsolicited visitors to the Kling Klang studio, it seems that occasional spiritual visitations were still welcome.

It therefore seems advisable to treat all Kraftwerk's declarations with a critical attitude, or at least a pinch of salt. To provide another example: despite claims that all the sounds on Kraftwerk records were self-produced, it now appears that the car noises at the beginning of 'Autobahn' – the ignition of an engine, followed by the stereoscopic sound of a car driving from left to right – were taken wholesale from a library record.[15]

Kraftwerk's refusal to re-release their first three albums is part of the creation of another myth – that of *Autobahn* being a kind of semi-miraculous *creatio ex nihilo*. Or take the lyrics of 'Computer World', rightly hailed as uncannily prophetic in predicting, among other things, the use of digital technology for business purposes. In the English version, there is a brief list of areas in which computers would indeed soon begin to play a crucial role: 'Business, numbers, money, people'.

These four terms, however, represent only a condensed version of the original German words, which run: 'Nummern, Zahlen, Handel, Leute, Reisen, Zeit, Medizin, Unterhaltung' ('Numbers, data, trade, people, travel, time, medicine, entertainment'). Now, as it happens, these eight words can be found in the list of categories in which the portable language-translator gadget from Texas

Instruments – owned by Florian Schneider – structures its vocabulary. Also, switch on a vintage Speak & Spell toy from the same company and you will hear a short melody very similar indeed to the beginning of 'Pocket Calculator'.

Equally, Ralf Hütter's various claims about the extraordinary amount of time the band supposedly spent in their artistic HQ cannot be taken literally: 'The 168-hour week is still going on since the beginning, since 1970,'[16] he bragged in 1991. The recollections by Karl Bartos, however, clearly contradict him in this respect. Better to take this assertion as an expression that the Kling Klang studio had been firmly at the centre of their creative lives.

Regarding the daily business of music production, Hütter is on record as saying: 'We play the machines and the machines play us. The machines should not do only slave work, we try to treat them as colleagues so they exchange energies with us.'[17] Such remarks relate to the notion of a man-machine symbiosis, and the site where this symbiosis flourishes is the Kling Klang studio, once called 'the mother ship' by Hütter.[18]

And the 'mother ship' was not for everybody. Unlike Andy Warhol's Factory, Kraftwerk operated behind closed doors, shutting out fans, journalists and other curious visitors. Even visitors such as

David Bowie or Brian Eno were not shown the studio; Hütter and Schneider took them to local cafés for their beloved coffee and cake instead. Inevitably, legendary stories about the Kling Klang studio began to circulate – such as the one about a strict ban on females (the idea behind this was to avoid the distraction that would, supposedly, inevitably ensue if girlfriends were present), or the one about the notorious telephone line that would never be answered (it was used only to make the most necessary external calls).

As Hütter once explained: 'The telephone is an antiquity – you never know who is calling, there is no image, it is an outmoded product which constantly disrupts work.'[19] Such secrecy and refusal to communicate were key in building the Kraftwerk myth. The less you say, the more people start to speculate, and the more interesting you get. This 'less is more' approach also served the band well during the later long, erratic periods in which they did not release any new music. You never know what to expect from Kraftwerk. And that remains true today.

Transatlantic Hybridizations: Afro-Germanic Beats

Here comes yet another mythical Kraftwerk tale – no doubt the most crucial as far as the question of legacy is concerned. It is the story of how the *industrielle Volksmusik* from Düsseldorf connected with the emerging black electronic-music scene in the United States. This wondrous story has often been told (and re-told), as befits every myth. In almost all versions, it is 'Planet Rock' by Afrika Bambaataa & The Soulsonic Force (released in 1988) that is identified as the decisive interface in this fusion. And rightly so.

Under the guidance of producer Arthur Baker, 'Planet Rock' sampled the brutal drum pattern of 'Numbers' and the distinctive melody of 'Trans-Europe Express', creating a funky take on the emerging electro sound. It was a futurist fantasy in which, according to academic Robert Fink, 'European art music is cast, consciously or not, in the role of an ancient, alien power source.'[20]

But this tale always limits the early influence of Kraftwerk on the electro and hip-hop communities of the West Coast. Many traces of the sound of Düsseldorf can be found in the pre-N.W.A. electro-rap and techno-pop scenes that emerged in LA between 1982 and 1987, including artists such as Egyptian Lover, Arabian Prince and the World Class Wreckin' Cru. They all developed a distinct West Coast fusion of Kraftwerk with other musical styles – especially the funk and soul of Prince and Rick James.

However, looking at the hybridization of two different cultures from a musical perspective is not the only option. It is more interesting to explore this synthesis from a different angle, identifying the trans-human notion governing *The Man-Machine* as the decisive cultural interface. Kraftwerk's decision to project a robot image of themselves was productively (mis)understood across the Atlantic as a move that consciously rejected identity definition along the (arbitrary) lines of nationality and skin colour.

The musical man-machine from Düsseldorf was perceived as a universal being, the harbinger of a future race that had overcome the confines of social division and discrimination. And that was quite an attractive proposition to African Americans. In the same way that Kraftwerk's music sought to reflect a specifically German identity (against the global dominance of Anglo-American music), the black communities in deprived inner-city areas developed their own styles in opposition to the rock mainstream of white America. The ruling musical paradigm from which both Kraftwerk and African-American minorities tried to distance themselves was essentially the same paradigm. And so was the common denominator which both parties shared: the increasingly rapid approach of the electronic production of music: future sounds made by machines. Anti-rock.

When Kraftwerk began to sense the growing interest in their music in the context of the disco explosion, they decided to make further inroads into the US music market with *The Man-Machine*. The African-American mixing engineer Leanard Jackson was flown in from Detroit. He was in for a surprise. According to Bussy, Jackson 'had arrived from America fully expecting to be assisting with an album made by four black guys from Düsseldorf. Having listened to their music, he was convinced that the basic rhythm tracks had to have been produced by black musicians.'[21]

This was a perfect example of an intercultural hybridization dissolving the notion of self-contained national characteristics. Kraftwerk had set out to create a distinctly German music and, by doing so, had inadvertently developed a type of sound which embodied national characteristics yet at the same time was fully compatible with an entirely different culture. A prominent witness who testified to the enthusiastic reception of Kraftwerk's indigenous electronic sound in the context of wholly different social and cultural milieus was Run DMC's Jam Master Jay: 'These guys proved to me you don't have to be where I'm from to get the music. That beat came from Germany all the way to the 'hoods of New York City.'[22]

To highlight how the exchange of cultural influences works in the context of electronic music, we need to return to Donna Summer's 'I Feel Love'. The epochal disco track appeared in 1978, the same year as *The Man-Machine*. It was produced in Munich by Italian-born Giorgio Moroder, who belonged to the German-speaking minority of the South Tyrol area of Italy. Moroder had made a number of solo albums with his studio musicians under the moniker Munich Machine; one of his tracks was even called 'Man Machine' (it would eventually become Blondie's 'Call Me').

Summer was born in Boston; her black father had been stationed as a GI in Germany and taught his wife to speak German. Summer herself became fluent in the language when she lived in Germany from 1968 to 1975, working as a singer. Moroder's production of 'I Feel Love' bore obvious similarities to the motorik beat sequences found on *Trans-Europe Express*. What made this disco hit so unique was its thoroughly innovative blend of diverse traditions and transnational influences: Summer and Moroder, who were both at the same time German and non-German, had produced a song blending African-American and German aesthetics, woman and machine.

Brian Eno agrees that Moroder's production

had a 'mechanical, Teutonic beat',[23] pointing to the rhythmic affiliation with Kraftwerk. Peter Shapiro described 'I Feel Love' as a 'masterpiece of mechanoeroticism'. Picking up on the Kraftwerk robot iconography, he links the track with the notion of the cyborg as an avatar for the overcoming of gender stereotypes: 'With songs like this [. . .], disco fostered an identification with the machine that can be read as an attempt to free gay men from the tyranny that dismisses homosexuality as an aberration, as a freak of nature.'[24]

Female R&B artist and actor Janelle Monáe could be cited as a more recent example of the cultural hybridizations that transmitted Kraftwerk's imagery across gender boundaries and national borders. The cover artwork for 2010's *The Arch-Android* shows a striking portrait of Monáe wearing an outlandish headpiece that strongly resembles the futuristic cityscape used by Kraftwerk on the 1975 tour posters on which the words 'Mensch-Maschine' first appeared. Monáe's otherworldly styling represents the android revolutionary Cindi Mayweather, whose story she narrates on this concept album.

The blueprint of Lang's *Metropolis* is evident, not least as Monáe released an EP named after the film in 2007, the cover of which featured her wearing an outfit that makes her look a lot like the female robot that features in the film. Monáe has repeatedly used female robot alter egos to express her androgyny, opaque sexual identity and gender fluidity, defying stereotypes of gender and race, just as her music crosses the boundaries of diverse styles such as hip-hop, new wave, funk, folk, rap and R&B. Her 2013 album was called *The Electric Lady* and, even though she has shed her transhuman imagery for her 2018 album, its title, *Dirty Computer*, once more establishes a link to the legacy of Kraftwerk. A funky female musical machine.

From Düsseldorf to Detroit and Back

As the history of techno shows, Kraftwerk's music was at the centre of the transnational exchange, validating the sometimes contested claim about the immense influence of their electronic robo-pop. The universal quality of the minimalist, repetitive music fell on particularly fertile soil with black producers in the Michigan industrial belt. They kick-started the new sound of Detroit in the early eighties, co-incidentally (or not) at about the same time that Kraftwerk's run of great albums essentially ground to a halt with *Computer World*.

Cybotron's seminal 'Clear' from 1983, for

instance, not only sounded as if it had emerged from the Kling Klang studio; even the band name owed a debt to Kraftwerk's robot aesthetics. Juan Atkins, the producer behind Cybotron, expertly adapted the sound from Germany, 'sometimes clearly referencing Kraftwerk tunes such as "Computer World" (on the track "Industrial Lies")'.[25] Alongside Kevin Saunderson and Derrick May, Atkins is revered as a pioneer of Detroit techno.[26]

Underground Resistance (UR), who belong to the so-called second wave of Detroit techno, were not only inspired by Kraftwerk's music but also amplified their artistic practices of secrecy and near-refusal to communicate with the outside world, forcing listeners to focus on the music itself. Founded in the early nineties, UR is both an independent record label and the *nom de plume* of Mike Banks and Jeff Mills. As Public Enemy overtly politicized rap, Banks and Mills did the same with techno music: UR understands itself as a collective whose members support themselves artistically as well as socially.

Although UR's radical politics differ from Kraftwerk's, their credo evidently connects with Kraftwerk's futuristic concerns and techno optimism, particularly prominent on *The Man-Machine*. Mike Banks explained why he and other

Detroit techno artists were so fascinated by Kraftwerk: 'In the early days, I never heard anybody say anything about their race. They weren't Germans, they weren't white, in fact we thought they were robots.'[27]

As one cultural historian writes, UR and other proponents of early Detroit techno strongly felt that 'racial identity should not be important to the valuation of music and the vision communicated through its sound, and – as the example of Kraftwerk demonstrates – that a sound and a visual politics which contest such identifications are progressive'.[28] Kraftwerk's fertile choice of the robot as their artistic image could also be taken as a 'declaration of an oblique solidarity with the hitherto put-upon not-quite-humans who had endured so much for so long. Hence the natural connection with African-American music and culture [. . .]. As white and male as they come, Kraftwerk were anti-white and anti-male in ways that mattered,'[29] concludes Stubbs.

It would be wrong, however, to limit the transnational influence of Kraftwerk to any one place with specific socio-economic structures such as Detroit. To posit that Kraftwerk were the originators of electronic dance music and the sole creative geniuses behind the concept of a future music would be equally wrong. Their futurist orientation proved instrumental in allowing their music to be re-codified in an entirely different cultural and social milieu, but that was only because there already existed a cultural tradition that pre-dated their artistic project: the phenomenon of Afro-futurism.

Although this term was coined in 1993 by the cultural critic Mark Dery, it refers to a literary and cultural aesthetic that appeared in the sixties. In terms of music, reference points often cited are the explicitly extraterrestrial mythologies of Sun Ra and his Arkestra, as well as George Clinton with Parliament-Funkadelic. Dery first defined Afro-futurism as: 'Speculative fiction that treats African themes and addresses African-American concerns in the context of twentieth century techno culture – and more generally, African-American signification that appropriates images of technology and a prosthetically enhanced future.'[30]

Critics have attributed the wider fascination with science fiction among the African-American community to the fact that African Americans had their heritage erased as a consequence of the crimes of the slave trade. As their cultural past is obscured and tainted by the collective trauma of their ancestors' forceful removal from their homelands, they are forced to look forward, towards a better future.

Structurally, this cultural mechanism is not

dissimilar to the situation faced by the generation of Germans to which Hütter and Schneider belong: in the same way that Kraftwerk's Germano-futurism offered a cultural perspective to deal with the moral dilemma of belonging to the guilty party, Afro-futurism offered an alternative vision to the descendants of the victims of the slave trade.

On the Aquabahn with Drexciya

A perfect example of a techno-music-based take on Afro-futurism is the production duo Drexciya. They were active during the nineties and operated under extreme levels of secrecy regarding the identity of the members. Drexciya's musical output is heavily influenced by Kraftwerk and constitutes a politically charged *Gesamtkunstwerk* based on the Afro-futurist legend of a hidden land called Drexciya on the seabed of the Atlantic.

According to the myth, Drexciya was founded by the children of African women who drowned in the Atlantic during the Middle Passage. (It was a common practice during the slave trade to throw pregnant women overboard, as they could not be sold on.) The babies, says the myth, continued to breathe underwater: first through amniotic fluid, then through lungs better suited to their aquatic world. They mature into a marine warrior race called Drexciyans, and they want to take their revenge.

The record releases by Drexciya presented themselves as messages from these underwater creatures, encoded in the universal language of techno music. For example, the cover artwork of their 1999 album, *Neptune's Lair*, depicts the metropolis of the subaquatic realm, while several subsequent releases feature the emblematic Drexciyan warrior, clad in a kind of diver suit and armed with a harpoon. Similarly, track titles refer to elements of Drexciyan mythology: 'Deep Sea Dweller', 'Quantum Hydrodynamics', 'Digital Tsunami', 'Aquatic Cataclysm' or indeed 'Aquabahn'.[31]

Most of Drexciya's releases appeared on the Berlin-based Tresor label. Tresor is connected to Germany's most famous techno club of the same name and one of its first releases was 'Sonic Destroyer' by Underground Resistance. Major releases, and indeed many true techno classics, are to be found on the Tresor label, among them X-102's 'Discovers the Rings of Saturn' (1992), Jeff Mills's 'Waveform Transmission Vol. 1' (1992), Robert Hood's 'Internal Empire' (1994), Drexciya's 'Neptune's Lair' (1999) or Shifted Phases' 'The Cosmic Memoirs of the Late Great Rupert J. Rosinthrope' (2002).

Both Tresor the club and the label have acted as

a vital conduit for the Berlin–Detroit axis, which was a driving force behind the boom of techno clubs in the German capital after the fall of the Berlin Wall in November 1989. The sound that Kraftwerk had helped to emerge in America had travelled back across the Atlantic and found a new home in the decrepit warehouses and deserted basement spaces of East Berlin. This concluded a cultural expedition in which their musical journeys structurally mimic the transatlantic voyages of the slave ships.

Kraftwerk paid homage to their spiritual brothers in *industrielle Volksmusik* with 'Planet of Visions', where, in the usual minimalist fashion, the musical affiliation is reduced to the words 'Detroit – Germany – We're so electro'. This was a greeting but also an invitation. The *Expo2000* EP of 1999, which contained three inhouse remixes of the title track, was followed in 2000 by a further remix EP.

Courtesy of Underground Resistance, *Expo Remix* features four blinding reworkings of the track. It was a gesture of reverence by the Detroit musicians and completed the circle of transatlantic musical exchange. Kraftwerk, in turn, used these versions as the basis of their live performances, as Hütter revealed: ' "Planet of Visions" incorporates their sounds into our show, so we're remixing their remixes of our mixes – it's feedback.'[32]

8. POSTSCRIPT: 1 2 3 4 5 6 7 8

The most recent new Kraftwerk studio material was released in 2003. With *Tour de France Soundtracks*, the band concluded a run of eight albums – the very octology that has been defined by the two *Catalogue* box sets as their œuvre. Eight is a pleasing, round number (in a numerological sense). It is perhaps for this reason that in the key track 'Numbers' from *Computer World* the robotic voice counts to eight (and not, say, to six or ten) against the background of thumping proto-techno.

Alongside 'Man-Machine', 'Numbers' is a popular Kraftwerk choice to open their set. One can assume that this has to do with their pride in demonstrating that, as far back as 1981, Kraftwerk were correctly predicting the future of electronic music. After all, the drum pattern was not just sampled by Afrika Bambaataa but also imitated by a host of other producers of African-American electronic music.

The key role of 'Numbers' now is that it inevitably makes an indirect reference to the canonical body of Kraftwerk's eight core albums from *Autobahn* to *Tour de France*. The prophetic song is hence at the centre of a dense conceptual interplay which connects the individual track not just with its host album, *Computer World*, but also with the wider Kraftwerk project.

If Kraftwerk were to release a ninth studio album, it would wreck the *Gesamtkunstwerk* that is the octology of the *Catalogue*-complex. Nine is neither eight nor ten but rather an ugly number, a misfit figure. Another studio album would feel like an appendage to the existing body of work. It is not least for this conceptual reason that I believe a ninth album will never see the light of day.

Another reason I doubt that we shall ever hear album number nine, despite Hütter's repeated claims that the band are slowly but steadily work-ing on it, is the lack of a suitable theme. To make it relevant, Kraftwerk would have to release an album that captures the very point of our societies' engage-ment with digital technology in a cutting-edge way. But today's world differs considerably from that of the seventies. It has developed a complexity which makes it exceptionally difficult to come up with a concept album that would epitomize an adequate response: genetic manipulation, digital capitalism, the dangerous rise of artificial intelligence, website algorithms manipulating our political views or con-sumer choices, the adverse effects of social media in general on society, to name just a few examples, do not really make for topics that warrant conceptualization in the form of a Kraftwerk album.

What one also needs to take into account is Ralf Hütter's negative stance towards digital lifestyles. As confessed in recent interviews, he is particularly critical of social media. When asked if he approved of Twitter, he replied: 'No, no, no. We just give information about our touring'; he rejected other social media pursuits, too: 'It's basically. . . very banal. Too much nonsense.'[1]

For all of these reasons, and maybe a few more, including, more prosaically, Hütter's age, I believe album number nine will never materialize – despite Hütter's ritual protestations that it will, at some unspecified future point. When questioned by an Irish newspaper journalist in 2013, he confirmed that work on a new release was ongoing: 'These things take time. We are a small independent unit. We are not Disney Studios or a large factory. But yes, the next step will be another album.'[2]

Now, maybe Hütter was simply misleading his interviewer to make him interpret his words as the promise of an upcoming studio album when in fact he was only referring to the *3-D The Catalogue* box set. In an interview from early 2015, Hütter displayed a degree of self-irony when replying to the default question about the release date of the next studio album: 'That is a difficult question, the answer usually runs: soon.'

But then there is no reason at all to complain. Kraftwerk are compensating for the lack of new studio material by vigorous touring, both in terms of the comprehensive *The Catalogue–12345678* retrospectives and their standard concerts, as well as shorter festival appearances and grand open-air shows. Given the immersive quality of their live appearances, it is only fair to say that the impressive audiovisual updates of their old releases are preferable to a potentially disappointing new studio album.

They also show no sign of preparing to retire – the German lyrics to 'Techno Pop' feature a message that is crucial to the Kraftwerk mission of making music: *'Es wird immer weiter geh'n/Musik als Träger von Ideen'* ('It will always go on from here/Music is the carrier of ideas'). Given that *industrielle Volksmusik* from Düsseldorf has become a crucial part of the DNA of electronic music, the groundbreaking idea of a new type of pop music developed by Ralf Hütter and Florian Schneider will indeed carry on and on. And on.

Towards the future of music.

ACKNOWLEDGEMENTS

I am indebted to many people I met along the way, ever since I began to make Kraftwerk into a subject of academic study.

Firstly, I have to thank Helen Conford for contacting me on the strength of my short review in the *Times Higher Education Supplement* of Morrissey's excellent novel, *List of the Lost*. How sad that Morrissey's books are now so much better than his music. A gnostic miracle.

Next, credit must go to Kraftwerk expert Klaus Zäpke for opening up the treasure trove of his Kraftwerk archive. He has always freely shared his in-depth knowledge with me, helping to eliminate many mistakes and misunderstandings on my part, not just in this book, but also elsewhere. Andréas Hagström did an excellent job as proofreader.

This introduction is based on the excellent foundation laid by the books written by the three Kraftwerk B-Boys: Barr, Bussy and Buckley. David Stubbs wrote the definitive book on Krautrock. Sean Albiez and David Pattie edited the groundbreaking first academic volume on Kraftwerk, which greatly inspired me.

The same applies to the fellow Kraftwerk researchers who contributed to the German volume I had the pleasure of editing: Ulrich Adelt, Heinrich Deisl, Pertti Grönholm, Marcus S. Kleiner, Didi Neidhart, Sean Nye, Melanie Schiller, Enno Stahl, Johannes Ullmaier and Jost Uhrmacher. Christoph Steker did a sterling job in copy-editing the volume.

Particular thanks to Enno Stahl's many efforts with the shorter version of the Kraftwerk conference he helped to organize in Düsseldorf in autumn 2015.

My friend, colleague and collaborator James Hodkinson is to be commended for his patience with me. I look forward to working with him on Kraftwerk, Krautrock and the rest.

Fellow Sebald scholar Scott Bartsch always replied quickly to queries regarding the intricate workings of the English language, while specialist librarian Richard Hopkins read through the entire manuscript to prevent me from submitting copy with embarrassing mistakes. Sarah Day and Shan Vahidy took excellent care with the various drafts this book has been through. Kevin Pocklington advised me expertly on all sorts of publishing matters.

Greetings to Rusty Egan, with particular thanks

for a blinding Kraftwerk set after the Kraftwerk conference; it was a true hammer-on-anvil affair. Always a pleasure to meet Thomas Meinecke, particularly on his trips to visit me in Birmingham. Greetings, too, to Kurt Dahlke a.k.a. Pyrolator, along with all regulars, for happy evenings in the POP Club. I enjoyed discussing Kraftwerk with Dylan enthusiast Heinrich Detering, who also made it possible for me to finally gain my *Habilitation* by talking about Kraftwerk's lyrics in Göttingen.

Emil Schult helped sort out communication with Kling Klang, as well as other Kraftwerk-related matters. Karl Bartos wrote an insightful book on his time with Kraftwerk and answered technical queries. Daniel Schneider from the Archiv der Jugendkulturen in Berlin-Kreuzberg procured rare reviews and features. Jens Strüver kindly DJed at several presentations of my German Kraftwerk book. Zeitkratzer leader Reinhold Friedl introduced me to the pleasures of Kraftwerk's early work.

As always, meeting with *Electri_City* maestro Rudi Esch and Propaganda mastermind Ralf Dörper from Düsseldorf in their hometown (but also elsewhere) was a pleasure. Andreas Spechtl joined me for an unpleasant Kraftwerk concert in stereo at the Birmingham Symphony Hall. Greetings to Mal and Suzie Rolfe in lovely Brighton.

I am aware, more acutely than ever, that this book, too, was written at the expense of spending time with my son, Lenz. That he could not join me for the Kraftwerk open-air concert in Düsseldorf on 1 July, celebrating the Grand Départ of the Tour de France 2017, was one of my many regrets of that year. However, the gigs we saw at the quarry in St Margarethen in 2018 and at the Arena in Vienna in 2019 more than made up for it.

My final and biggest gratitude, as always, to my wife, Antje, for copy-editing, and even more for her patience and love.

NOTES

Foreword

1 Wolfgang Flür's rambling and not very well-written memoir was the subject of a lawsuit by Hütter and Schneider upon its original publication in German in 1999. The ensuing ban related only to Germany; the later English version was not covered by the court order. An updated version, which made the book far more readable, appeared in 2017. Unlike Bartos, Flür did not use diaries but reconstructs anecdotal events from memory.

1. Introduction: The Birth of Electronic Pop Music in Düsseldorf

1 Mark Fisher, *Ghosts of My Life: Writings on Depression, Hauntology and Lost Futures* (Winchester, 2014), p. 9.

2 David Buckley, *Kraftwerk: Publikation* (London, 2012), p. 126.

3 For more on Laibach see Daniela Kirschsteiner, Johann Lughofer and Uwe Schütte (eds.), *Gesamtkunstwerk Laibach: Klang, Bild, Politik* (Klagenfurt, 2018).

4 Quoted in Pascal Bussy, *Kraftwerk: Man, Machine and Music* (London, 2001), p. 23.

5 Quoted in Tim Barr, *Kraftwerk: From Düsseldorf to the Future (with Love)* (London, 1998), p. 142.

6 Quoted in Paul Alessandrini, 'Haute Tension'. Interview with Ralf Hütter and Florian Schneider, *Rock & Folk*, 11 (1976), p. 54.

7 Christoph Dallach, 'Die Maschinen spielen uns'. Interview with Ralf Hütter, *Der Spiegel*, 13 July 2003.

8 Markus Meyer, 'Werk mit Kraft', *Süddeutsche Zeitung*, 7 September 2000.

9 Matthias Schönebäumer, 'Minimal Emotional', *Die Zeit*, 12 January 2009.

10 Tobias Rüther, 'Die Stimme der Energie', *Frankfurter Allgemeine Zeitung*, 7 January 2009.

11 Alexis Petridis, 'Desperately Seeking Kraftwerk', *Guardian*, 25 July 2003.

12 Cf. http://pitchfork.com/reviews/albums/4557-minimum-maximum.

13 Paul Alessandrini, Interview with Ralf Hütter and Florian Schneider, *Rock & Folk*, 11 (1976).

14 Quoted in Barr, *Kraftwerk*, p. 64.

15 Barr, *Kraftwerk*, p. 8.

16 Ibid., p. 7.

17 Quoted in Rob Young, *All Gates Open: The Story of Can* (London, 2018), p. 369.

18 Another fine example would be the British-based German writer W. G. Sebald, who quickly turned into a literary star in the English-speaking world following the publication of his story collection *The Emigrants* in 1996, while his books were met with reservation and criticism in his native country.

19 Quoted in Buckley, *Kraftwerk*, p. 45.

20 Chris Petit, '*Am Diskö mit Kraftwerk*' , in Uwe Schütte (ed.), *Mensch-Maschine-Musik: Das Gesamtkunstwerk Kraftwerk* (Düsseldorf, 2018), pp. 116–23.

21 Quoted in Bussy, *Kraftwerk*, p. 164.

22 Quoted in Alexander Simmeth, *Krautrock transnational: Die Neuerfindung der Popmusik in der BRD, 1968–1978* (Bielefeld, 2013) p. 259.

23 Willi Andresen, 'Computer Liebe'. Interview with Ralf Hütter, *Tip*, 22 (1991), p. 202.

24 *Heimat*, in Germany, is a concept that is not adequately rendered by translating it as 'homeland'. In the German cultural imagination, it has a strongly nostalgic edge and denotes a sense of belonging steeped in one's individual family history. The Nazis misused the notion by giving it overtones of ethnic purity, which is why it became tainted and contested after 1945.

25 Michael Bracewell, 'Wired for Sound'. Interview with Ralf Hütter, *Frieze Magazine*, 98 (2006).

26 Ibid.

27 Cf. http://www.simsi.net/4680/4734.html. Many Futurists were later associated with the Italian branch of fascism and supported Benito Mussolini, Hitler's political ally. Hütter and Schneider will undoubtedly have been aware of this development and certainly did not approve of this political aspect when praising Futurism.

28 Cf. https://frieze.com/article/wired-sound.

29 Gene R. Swenson, 'What is Pop Art? Answers from 8 Painters', *Art News*, 62 (1963).

30 Mark Dery, Interview with Ralf Hütter, *Keyboard* magazine, 10 (1991).

31 Quoted in Rudi Esch, *Electri_City: The Düsseldorf School of Electronic Music* (London, 2016), p. 116.

32 Quoted in Buckley, *Kraftwerk*, p. 89.

33 Andresen, 'Computer Liebe', p. 202.

34 As in the case of, say, Detroit, Birmingham or Sheffield, where the existence of heavy industry provided the real-life economic background for the development of sonically related musical styles – such as proto-punk (The Stooges), heavy metal (Black Sabbath) and experimental industrial (Cabaret Voltaire) – Kraftwerk succeeded in transforming the industrial sounds of pulsating noise and metal clanging from the Rhine-Ruhr area into a thoroughly modern music.

2. Early Works: The Kraftwerk Story Unfolds

1 Quoted in Ed Power, 'Ghost in the Machine', *Independent* (Ireland), 12 July 2013.

2 The label was founded in 1975 to release their fifth album, *Radio-Activity*, in the same year.

3 David Pattie, 'Kraftwerk: Playing the Machines', in Sean Albiez and David Pattie (eds.), *Kraftwerk: Music Non-Stop* (London, 2011), p. 128.

4 German civilians who had experienced the obliteration of Hamburg, Cologne and other major cities were normally too traumatized to talk about it, and certainly

not in public. As W. G. Sebald has shown in his book *On the Natural History of Destruction* (2003), there existed a wide-ranging taboo on the mass killings of 'non-combatants', so these were largely perceived as a sort of retribution for the many terrible atrocities the Nazis had committed in the extermination camps and, along with the German army, during the war in Eastern Europe.

5 Quoted in Pascal Bussy, *Kraftwerk: Man, Machine and Music* (London, 2001), p. 21.

6 Quoted in David Stubbs, *Mars by 1980: The Story of Electronic Music* (London, 2018), p. 225.

7 Quoted in Tim Barr, *Kraftwerk: From Düsseldorf to the Future (with Love)* (London, 1998), p. 74.

8 Kraftwerk would repeat this trick on later releases, for instance 'Europe Endless' on *Trans-Europe Express*.

9 Neu!'s first three amazing albums – *Neu!* (1972), *Neu! 2* (1973), *Neu! 75* (1975) – can be seen as a spin-off from the propulsive sound forged by Dinger and Rother as Kraftwerk's rhythm section. Their music also pre-empted Kraftwerk's later turn to forward-thrusting rhythm, albeit through a mixture of electronics and guitar sounds.

10 The concert at the so-called *Karussell für die Jugend* (Merry-go-round for Youth) was an attempt to lure young people away from the lurid, alcohol-fuelled pleasures of the annual Kirmes festival. Concert tickets were cheap and subsidized soft drinks were on offer. When the city administration joined in cooperation with the WDR, the broadcaster paid for interesting new local bands to appear for the TV broadcast, and among them were Kraftwerk and Can, so the audience included both

long-haired hippie types in woollen jumpers, as well as more intellectual types with tie and jacket. Similarly, reactions to Kraftwerk's performance differed enormously, ranging from bemused but distant curiosity to excited head-banging.

11 The inferior artwork of the British pressing was vastly different from the original, showing simply a brownish circuit board with the band name and title in red letters.

12 Quoted in Barr, *Kraftwerk*, p. 156.

13 David Buckley, *Kraftwerk: Publikation* (London, 2012), p. 47.

14 Carsten Brocker, 'Kraftwerk: Technology and Composition', in Albiez and Pattie (eds.), *Kraftwerk*, p. 103.

15 Buckley, *Kraftwerk*, p. 46.

16 Quoted in Bussy, *Kraftwerk*, p. 43.

17 Ibid., p. 23.

18 Quoted in Barr, *Kraftwerk*, p. 75.

3. Movement and Velocity: From *Autobahn* to *Trans-Europe Express*

1 Lester Bangs, 'Kraftwerkfeature', in *Psychotic Reactions and Carburettor Dung: The Work of a Legendary Critic: Rock'n'Roll as Literature and Literature as Rock'n'Roll* (New York, 1988), p. 158.

2 Brian Eno famously decreed: 'There were three great beats in the seventies: Fela Kuti's Afrobeat, James Brown's funk and Klaus Dinger's Neu! beat.' (Quoted in Lloyd Isaac Vayo, 'What's Old is NEU!: Benjamin Meets

Rother and Dinger', in *Popular Music and Society*, 32:5 (2009), p. 621).

3 Quoted in Albert Koch, 'Unsere Musik ist wie ein Filmskript'. Interview with Ralf Hütter, *Musikexpress*, 4 (2019), p. 50.

4 Quoted in Stephen Dalton, 'Album by Album: Kraftwerk', *Uncut*, 9 (2009), p. 68.

5 Sean Albiez and Kyre Tromm Lindvig, ' "Autobahn" and Heimatklänge: Soundtracking the FRG', in Sean Albiez and David Pattie (eds.), *Kraftwerk: Music Non-Stop* (London, 2011), p. 39.

6 Flür, quoted in Rudi Esch, *Electri_City: The Düsseldorf School of Electronic Music* (London, 2016), p. 90.

7 Chris Bohn, 'The Autobahn Goes on Forever', in Robert Young (ed.), *Undercurrents: The Hidden Wiring of Modern Music* (London, 2002), p. 143.

8 Quoted in ibid., p. 145.

9 Quoted in Pascal Bussy, *Kraftwerk: Man, Machine and Music* (London, 2001), p. 161.

10 The curious spelling of the title of the interview probably relates to the ability of the German language to form composite nouns (i.e. *Kraftwerkartikel*).

11 Bangs, 'Kraftwerkfeature', p. 154.

12 Ibid., p. 157.

13 Ibid., p. 158.

14 Tim Barr, *Kraftwerk: From Düsseldorf to the Future (with Love)* (London, 1998), p. 91.

15 Bangs, 'Kraftwerkfeature', p. 159.

16 *Circus*, 6 (1975).

17 *Billboard*, 11 January 1975.

18 *Cash Box*, 11 January 1975.

19 Hans-Joachim Krüger, 'Kraftwerk – Autobahn', in *Sounds*, 70 (1974), p. 44.

20 N.N., 'Trance-Musik: Schamanen am Synthesizer', *Der Spiegel*, 20 (1975).

21 Christoph Amend, 'Und plötzlich standen wir in einem elektronischen Garten'. Interview with Ralf Hütter, *Zeit* magazine, 18 May 2017, pp. 14–23.

22 Paul Alessandrini, 'Haute Tension'. Interview with Ralf Hütter and Florian Schneider, *Rock & Folk*, 11 (1976).

23 Karl Bartos, *Der Klang der Maschine* (Eichborn, 2017), p. 170.

24 Quoted in Bussy, *Kraftwerk*, p. 64.

25 Bartos, *Der Klang der Maschine*, p. 194.

26 Quoted in Bussy, *Kraftwerk*, p. 155.

27 Urich Adelt, *Krautrock: German Music in the Seventies* (Michigan, 2016), p. 27.

28 David Stubbs, *Future Days: Krautrock and the Building of Modern Germany* (London, 2014), pp. 179–80.

29 Wolfgang Flür, *I was a Robot* (London, 2017), pp. 96–7.

30 Greil Marcus, *The History of Rock 'n' Roll in Ten Songs* (New Haven, 2014), p .33.

31 For example, experimental composer Heiner Goebbels and East German playwright Heiner Müller, as well as the writer Thomas Meinecke and producer Move D,

have collaborated on some remarkable experimental pieces. Noteworthy also are the radio plays by Hamburg musician Felix Kubin, whose work displays some evident influences by Kraftwerk; see for example his 2018 work, *Die Maschine steht still* (*The Machine Stops*), based on a short story by E. M. Forster.

32 Ingeborg Schober, interview with Ralf Hütter, *Musikexpress*, 12 (1976).

33 Hans Ulrich Obrist, 'Augen zu und hören, hören, hören'. Interview with Karlheinz Stockhausen, in Imke Misch (ed.), *Texte zur Musik 1998–2007: KLANG-Zyklus, Geist und Musik* (Kürten, 2014), p. 273.

34 Quoted in Barr, *Kraftwerk*, p. 46.

35 Quoted in Albiez and Pattie (eds.), *Kraftwerk*, p. 34.

36 Mark Dery, interview with Ralf Hütter, *Keyboard Magazine*, 10 (1991).

37 The brooch made its first appearance on the cover image of *Ralf and Florian*. On the English version of *Trans-Europe Express*, a second, similarly old-fashioned-looking band photo can be found. It was taken by the photographer J. Stara in Paris. His group-portrait technique was to take individual shots of each member, using static lighting and from fixed perspectives. The final image was a retouched and colourized montage of the individual portraits. As a result of this outmoded method, the head of Florian Schneider looked a little larger than it should be, giving the band portrait an air of artificiality.

38 Hagström (ed.), *Influences, References and Imitations*, p. 120.

39 Quoted in Barr, *Kraftwerk*, p. 93.

40 Doug Lynner and Bryce Robbley, 'A Conversation with Ralf Hütter and Florian Schneider of Kraftwerk', *Synapse* 9/10 (1976), pp. 10–11.

41 Initially, the Schengen zone just covered Germany, France and the Benelux countries; from 1990, it included most membership countries. (The UK refused to sign up.)

42 Quoted in Alessandrini, 'Haute Tension'.

43 Quoted in Hillegonda Rietveld, ' "Trans-Europe Express": Tracing the Trance Machine', in Albiez and Pattie (eds.), *Kraftwerk*, p. 216.

44 Quoted in Bussy, *Kraftwerk*, p. 90.

45 Quoted in Alessandrini, 'Haute Tension' .

46 Quoted in Bussy, *Kraftwerk*, p. 87.

47 Bussy, *Kraftwerk*, p. 89.

48 Quoted in Alessandrini, 'Haute Tension'.

49 Irritatingly, there is a stopover in Vienna, which of course means quite a detour; it would only constitute a 'straight connection', as the lyrics claim, if you were travelling on two separate services. In any case, the Café Hawelka in Dorotheergasse near St Stephen's Cathedral was deemed always worth a visit by Hütter and Schneider. Run by Leopold and Josefine Hawelka since 1945, it was famous for being Vienna's premier hang-out for artists, writers, intellectuals and journalists. Hütter and Schneider are known for their passion for coffee and cake, regularly haunting the cafés near the Kling Klang studio. At the Hawelka, they will have tucked into tasty *Buchteln*, yeast dumplings with plum purée, an Austrian speciality.

50 Quoted in Alessandrini, 'Haute Tension'.

51 We know about anecdotes such as Florian Schneider taking his former idol Iggy Pop asparagus shopping (which is a kind of German ritual in asparagus season). We don't know for sure, though, why the much-discussed collaboration between Kraftwerk and Bowie never materialized. The most likely reason would have been that Hütter and Schneider felt that any such collaboration, as flattering as it was, given Bowie's standing as a musician, would damage the integrity of the Kraftwerk concept. After all, they turned down Michael Jackson, too. (Luckily for him – Jackson went on to Quincy Jones, who produced *Thriller* for him.) According to Bartos, Elton John was also keen to work with Kraftwerk.

52 Quoted in Rietveld, ' "Trans-Europe Express" ', p. 215.

53 Flür, *I was a Robot*, pp. 126–7.

54 Bartos, *Der Klang der Maschine*, pp. 222–3.

55 Quoted in Stubbs, *Future Days*, p. 189.

56 Stubbs, ibid.

57 Quoted in David Toop, *Rap Attack: African Jive to New York Hip Hop* (New York, 1984), p. 130.

58 Alessandrini, 'Haute Tension'.

59 Quoted in Barr, *Kraftwerk*, p. 127.

60 The first performance by Laibach outside of Yugoslavia took place in 1987 at the exhibition *Was ist Kunst?*, which was held at Galerie Möbel Perdu in Hamburg. The gallery was run by Florian Schneider's sister Claudia Schneider-Esleben, establishing an early connection between the two bands.

61 Ware, quoted in Esch, *Electri_City*, p. 161.

62 Quoted in Alessandrini, 'Haute Tension'.

4. 'We are the Robots': From *The Man-Machine* to *Computer World*

1 Quoted in Andreas Hagström (ed.), *Influences, References and Imitations: On the Aesthetes of Kraftwerk* (Gothenburg, 2015), p. 115.

2 Pascal Bussy, *Kraftwerk: Man, Machine and Music* (London, 2001), p. 93.

3 David Stubbs, *Future Days: Krautrock and the Building of Modern Germany* (London, 2014), p. 192.

4 Rudi Esch, *Electri_City: The Düsseldorf School of Electronic Music* (London, 2016), p. 177.

5 Andy Gill, 'Mind Machine Music', *NME*, 29 April 1978.

6 David Buckley, *Kraftwerk: Publikation* (London, 2012), p. 145.

7 It may have been for this reason that the song's chart success only came three years after the release of *Man-Machine*. Originally, the song was on the B-side of the UK 'Computer Love' single released in July 1981. When it turned out that 'The Model' proved more popular on radio play than the A-side, the song was reissued in December 1981. Only after this erratic journey, with it finally becoming available in the UK as the A-side, did it reach its number-one chart position in February 1982.

8 One may want to argue, Though, that the song portrays the modelling profession as get another form of a

(wo)man-machine-like work, where the female human is forced to adopt the role of an artificial person, standing immovable while being photographed.

9   The instrumental 'Spacelab' reflected the habit of space-faring nations of launching laboratories into the Earth's orbit. Wernher von Braun had advocated the idea in a number of articles published in the early fifties. While not a Nazi politically, he had closely cooperated with Hitler's regime in order to fulfil his ambitions as a space-travel engineer. Braun's interest in rockets was specifically for their use in space travel, not as weapons. Still, Braun was personally promoted to the rank of professor by Hitler for his work on the V2 rocket, which the Nazis had hoped would destroy large parts of London. After the war, he was one of many German scientists co-opted by the US Joint Intelligence Objectives Agency to work for the US government: false employment histories were created, and their regime affiliations expunged from the public record. With their records bleached, the former Nazi collaborators were ready to work for their new employers. Braun had an exemplary career at NASA and died, an American citizen, in 1977. In 1959, he submitted the plans for a project codenamed Project Horizon to the US army. It detailed an orbiting laboratory to serve as basis for research and further explorations of space. The first such space station was the Skylab operated by NASA and sent into orbit in 1973. In the following year, the construction of the European Spacelab project began; its first missions were flown in 1981 and 1982. Being the only Kraftwerk track to deal with space exploration as an advanced form of travel, it was a stunning coup when at a concert in Stuttgart in July 2018 there was a live link

to the International Space Station, allowing the German astronaut (and Kraftwerk fan) Alexander Gerst to speak directly to the concert audience, declaring 'The ISS is a man-machine, the most complex and valuable machine humankind has ever built.' His surprise appearance segued into the performance of 'Spacelab', during which live footage from inside and outside of the ISS was transmitted on the stage screen.

10 Quoted in Stubbs, *Future Days*, p. 173.

11 Another possible source, as Andréas Hagström found out, could have been Emil Schult. He must have come across an article about 'The Man-Machine concept' published in an issue of *Design Quarterly* from 1967, since he used clippings from that magazine in an artist's book he published in 1976. (Cf. Andréas Hagström, *Em Fest für die Sinne: An Aesthetic History*, in: Hagström (ed.), *Influences, References and Imitations*, pp. 105–34 (115).)

12 Quoted in Tim Barr, *Kraftwerk: From Düsseldorf to the Future (with Love)* (London, 1998), p. 7.

13 What makes *Metropolis* relevant in regard to the Kraftwerkian predilection for all things ambivalent is that it is problematic and deeply ambivalent itself. Film critic Siegfried Kracauer branded it proto-fascist in his book *From Caligari to Hitler* (1947). The plot is confused in terms of its politics: it shows how the rising revolutionary antagonism between the proletarian masses and the privileged class ruling Metropolis is defused through the intervention of a 'facilitator'/'mediator'. Kracauer understood this figure as an analogy to Hitler. Hitler likewise sought to stabilize the volatile political tensions in Germany after the First World War by channelling them into

his nationalist, racist policies of uniting the proletariat and the well-off under the banner of a Greater German Empire. Scriptwriter Thea von Harbou later joined the Nazis, while Fritz Lang went into exile in America.

14 Instead of them, it was their disco competitor Giorgio Moroder who provided the new music to a bowdlerized version of the film released in 1984 – a truly dreadful pop soundtrack featuring eighties artists such as Adam Ant, Pat Benatar and Bonnie Tyler. A more fitting musical score, however, was released by Detroit techno artist Jeff Mills in 2000. Krautrock legend Dieter Moebius, too, composed a soundtrack for the movie which was posthumously released as *Musik für Metropolis* in 2017.

15 Simon Witter, 'Paranoid Androids?'. Interview with Ralf Hütter, *Mojo* 9 (2005), p. 51. Contrary to what is suggested in the quote, there is, of course, nothing specifically French about retro-futurism.

16 Quoted in Mark Sinker and Tim Barr, 'Electro kinetik', in Chris Kempster (ed.), *History of House* (London, 1996), p. 96.

17 Quoted in Bussy, *Kraftwerk*, p. 96.

18 Ibid., p. 99.

19 Philip Warkander, 'The Mechanical Body: Kraftwerk and Contemporary Fashion', in Hagström (ed.), *Influences, References and Imitations*, pp. 183–90.

20 Quoted in Bussy, *Kraftwerk*, p. 155.

21 Riccardo Campa, *Humans and Automata. A Social Study of Robotics* (Frankfurt, 2015), p. 23.

22 David Pattie, 'Kraftwerk: Playing the Machines', in Sean Albiez and David Pattie (eds.), *Kraftwerk: Music Non-Stop* (London, 2011), pp. 125–6.

23 Quoted in Bussy, *Kraftwerk*, p. 154.

24 Quoted in Buckley, *Kraftwerk*, p. 130.

25 Quoted in Buckley, *Kraftwerk*, p. 94.

26 EMI press release on *Computer World*, quoted in Urich Adelt, *Krautrock: German Music in the Seventies* (Michigan, 2016), p. 30.

27 Stubbs, *Future Days*, p. 194.

28 Quoted in Buckley, *Kraftwerk*, p. 130.

29 She is the wife of Masayuki Akamatsu, who developed the generative app *Minicomposer* with Karl Bartos.

30 Quoted in Witter, 'Paranoid Androids?', p. 52.

31 Quoted in Bussy, *Kraftwerk*, p. 125.

32 Tellingly, this typographical feature was kept for the graphic-design overhaul that was part of *The Catalogue* in 2009.

33 Stubbs, *Future Days*, p. 204.

34 David Cunningham, 'Kraftwerk and the Image of the Modern', in Albiez and Pattie (eds.), *Kraftwerk*, p. 47.

35 Quoted in Buckley, *Kraftwerk*, p. 93.

36 Ibid., p. 169.

37 The gadget in question was the frequency shifter invented by the renowned engineer Harald Bode. With it, you could raise or lower the frequency of the music input signal, resulting in a more metallic-sounding effect.

38 Quoted in Barr, *Kraftwerk*, p. 74.

39 Elizabeth Guffey and Kate C. Lemay, 'Retrofuturism and Steampunk', *The Oxford Handbook to Science Fiction* (Oxford, 2014), p. 434.

40 Bussy, *Kraftwerk*, p. 114.

41 Alexei Monroe, '*Computer World* Now and Then. The Revolutionary Influence of Kraftwerk', *Trebuchet* 3 (2018), p. 52.

42 Ibid., p. 51.

43 Karl Bartos, *Der Klang der Maschine* (Eichborn, 2017), p. 267.

44 Neil Rowland, 'Electronic Zeitgeist'. Interview with Ralf Hütter, *Melody Maker*, 4 July 1981.

45 Pertti Grönholm, 'When Tomorrow Began Yesterday: Kraftwerk's Nostalgia for the Past Futures', in *Popular Music and Society*, 38, (2015), pp. 373–4.

46 Ibid., p. 372.

47 The remastered soundtrack has gained cult status in Germany and was reissued several times, most recently in 2010.

48 Jean Eric Perrin, 'Komputer'. Interview with Ralf Hütter, *Rock & Folk*, 178 (1981).

49 Quoted in Barr, *Kraftwerk*, p. 155.

50 Pattie, 'Kraftwerk: Playing the Machines', p. 131.

51 Quoted in Barr, *Kraftwerk*, p. 152.

52 Quoted in Bussy, *Kraftwerk*, p. 113.

53 The running order of songs and the length of sets differed between the various locations. Generally, about

eighteen songs were played, but concerts could be as short as thirteen songs (for instance, at the Alte Oper, Frankfurt, on 9 December 1981) or indeed run to a lavish twenty-two-song set, such as on 23 August 1981 at the beautiful open-air venue Opera Leśna in Sopot, Poland. The long set featured several tracks from *Radio-Activity* and the B-side of *Autobahn*. It also included a song from that period which was never officially released and was unveiled during concerts in 1975, 'Die Sonne, der Mond, die Sterne' ('The Sun, the Moon, the Stars'). Lasting a little under three minutes, it is a quiet, atmospheric mood piece based on organ chords with added electronic noises and vocoder-vocals repeating the title and would have been a perfect fit on *Radio-Activity*.

54 Bussy, *Kraftwerk*, p. 115.

55 Quoted in ibid.

5. Enter the Digital Revolution: From *Techno Pop* to *Tour de France*

1 Hütter and Schneider also considered the title *Techni-color* but had to abandon their plans due to potential copyright infringement of the US film technology company of the same name.

2 Sean Nye, 'Von "Electric Café" zu "Techno Pop": Versuch einer Kritik eingefahrener Rezeptionsmuster', in Uwe Schütte (ed.): *Mensch-Maschinen-Musik: Das Gesamtkunstwerk Kraftwerk* (C. W. Leske, 2018), pp. 140–56 (141–2).

3   James Henke, 'Yellow Magic Orchestra: Japanese Tech-
    nopop is Poised to Invade America', *Rolling Stone* (US),
    12 June 1980.

4   Cf. Pascal Bussy, *Kraftwerk: Man, Machine and Music*
    (London, 2001), p. 132.

5   The track also appears as 'Music Non Stop' for no appar-
    ent reason, so it seems to be more a case of sloppiness
    than any conceptual depth to the interchangeability
    between French and English spelling.

6   Quoted in Rudi Esch, *Electri_City: The Düsseldorf School
    of Electronic Music* (London, 2016), p. 362.

7   This moment is probably a reference to the famous scene
    in Lang's movie *Metropolis* in which the robot first opens
    its eyes as it comes alive.

8   David Buckley, *Kraftwerk: Publikation* (London, 2012),
    p. 213.

9   Nye, 'Von "Electric Café" zu "Techno Pop"', p. 146.

10 Bartos had originally suggested Henning Schmitz, later
    also to become part of the Kraftwerk live line-up, replac-
    ing Bartos, but Schmitz originally declined and in turn
    recommended Hilpert.

11 Quoted in Bussy, *Kraftwerk*, p. 150.

12 The artwork on the inside of the gatefold, however, did
    show a group of four robot dummies. But strangely
    enough, Flür and Bartos were replaced by two robots,
    each sporting Fritz Hilpert's face. Later promotional
    photos showed a robot head imitating short-lived Kraft-
    werk recruit Fernando Abrantes, who was a temporary
    replacement following the departure of Karl Bartos.

13 Quoted in Bussy, *Kraftwerk*, p. 156.

14 Quoted in Tim Barr, *Kraftwerk: From Düsseldorf to the Future (with Love)* (London, 1998), p. 155.

15 Barr, ibid., p. 39.

16 (No name), 'The Future is Virtual'. Music tech talk with Fritz Hilpert, *Sounds & Performance*, 2009.

17 Cf. Karl Bartos, *Der Klang der Maschine* (Eichborn, 2017), pp. 307–10.

18 Tobias Rapp and Frank Thadeusz, 'Maschinen sind einfach lockerer', *Der Spiegel*, 50 (2009), p. 140.

19 Fred Durst, 'Kraftwerk: Iederen houdt van herhaling', *Humo* 8 (2003), pp. 160–61.

20 Ibid.

21 For example, the track featured in the US hip-hop movie *Breakin'* (1984) but appeared only as a cover version on the soundtrack, was then reissued in 1999 and appeared, in a newly recorded version, on the *Tour de France Soundtracks* album in 2003. In addition to these releases, it also materialized as a remix by Karl Bartos in 1998 and featured on the soundtrack to the video game *Wipeout 2048* in 2014.

22 Cf. http://www.spiegel.de/kultur/musik/expo-der-400-000-mark-jingle-a-30536.html.

23 Quoted in Bussy, *Kraftwerk*, p. 125.

24 Cf. http://twingokraftwerk.com/news/alohainterview2004/20040803-alohainterview.html.

25 Geeta Dayal, 'Kraftwerk on Cycling, 3D, "Spiritual Connection" to Detroit'. Interview with Ralf Hütter, *Rolling Stone* (US), 8 (2015).

26 Hindemith may be more important for Kraftwerk than so far recognized. His notion of *Gebrauchsmusik* (utility music/music for use) bears an evident proximity to the concept of *industrielle Volksmusik*. Hindemith's compositions of the Weimar period were a reaction against the elitism associated with professional virtuoso music. Rather, they constituted a type of music that is aesthetically sophisticated yet can be performed by talented amateurs by virtue of its simplicity of technique and style.

27 Klaus Totzler, interview with Ralf Hütter, *Skug online*, 26 May 2004. Given that rap was well under way in 1983, his claim can be considered another example of Kraftwerk's self-constructed myth-making.

28 Dayal, 'Kraftwerk on Cycling'.

29 Cf. http://twingokraftwerk.com/news/alohainterview 2004/20040803-alohainterview.html.

30 Dayal, 'Kraftwerk on Cycling'.

31 Cf. http://twingokraftwerk.com/news/alohainterview 2004/20040803-alohainterview.html.

32 Quoted in Buckley, *Kraftwerk*, p. 249.

33 Ibid., p. 251.

34 They also issued a DVD set with surround-sound mixes and a SuperAudio-CD edition for fans who owned the necessary equipment. The SA–CD now commands very high prices among collectors.

35 The very first concert in this stage arrangement was played in Ghent in 2002.

36 Quoted in Buckley, *Kraftwerk*, p. 262.

6. Sound and Vision 3D: Working on *The Catalogue*

1 Quoted in David Buckley, *Kraftwerk: Publikation* (London, 2012), pp. 76–7.

2 Kraftwerk even provided sounds and vocals based on 'Music Non Stop' for the intro to the MTV programme of the same name, as well as short jingles that were shown throughout the programme. The colourful, crudely animated computer-generated images bear, however, only little proximity to Kraftwerk's visual aesthetics. Cf. https://www.youtube.com/watch?v=4NwAdUojggA

3 Worth a mention in this context is that already in April 1971 Kraftwerk had done a performance accompanying a 3D laser show by the Swedish artist Carl-Fredrik Reuterswärd at the Kunsthalle Düsseldorf. The two-hour extravaganza was attended by some 2,000 people. However, this was during the period when Hütter had temporarily left the band.

4 Arno Frank, 'Perfektion Mekanik Aero Dynamik'. Interview with Ralf Hütter, *Der Spiegel*, 30 May 2017.

5 Quoted in Buckley, *Kraftwerk*, p. 143.

6 David Pattie, 'Kraftwerk: Playing the Machines', in Sean Albiez and David Pattie (eds.), *Kraftwerk, Music Non-Stop* (London, 2011), p. 119.

7 Quoted in Tim Barr, *Kraftwerk: From Düsseldorf to the Future (with Love)* (London, 1998), p. 157.

8   Kraftwerk used Sony VAIO laptops in an interesting deviation from the dominance of Apple MacBooks in electronic music.

9   Klaus Totzler, interview with Ralf Hütter, *Skug online*, 26 May 2004.

10 Ibid.

11 Ibid.

12 Michael Bracewell, 'Wired for Sound'. Interview with Ralf Hütter, *Frieze* magazine, 98 (2006).

13 Quoted in Buckley, *Kraftwerk*, p. 75.

14 Cf. http://www.electronicbeats.net/emil-schult-on-kraftwerk.

15 Ibid.

16 Quoted in Barr, *Kraftwerk*, p. 71.

17 Ibid., p. 75.

18 Quoted in Pascal Bussy, *Kraftwerk: Man, Machine and Music* (London, 2001), p. 48.

19 Even the video for the 1986 single 'The Telephone Call' was still done in the black-and-white aesthetic, despite the fact that it was an evident mismatch with the digital cover artwork. Or simply call it retro-futurism.

20 Speculation would point to a disagreement between Hütter and Schneider, or potential dissatisfaction about the sound quality of some of the remasters. Quite likely it was also a business decision – with the band on tour in 2004 promoting *Tour de France Soundtracks* (2003) and a live album in the pipeline for 2005, it would have been

indeed ridiculous if Kraftwerk had been flooding the market with yet another major release.

21 Cf. http://www.electronicbeats.net/thomas-demand-recommends-kraftwerk-3d.

22 Cf. http://www.peterboettcher.de/en/kraftwerk.html.

23 Quoted in Buckley, *Kraftwerk*, p. 274.

24 Cf. http://www.simsi.net/4680/4734.html.

7. 'Music Non-Stop': Kraftwerk's Legacy

1   Quoted in Tim Barr, *Kraftwerk: From Düsseldorf to the Future (with Love)* (London, 1998), p. 154.

2   Quoted in David Stubbs, *Future Days: Krautrock and the Building of Modern Germany* (London, 2014), p. 205.

3   Quoted in Pascal Bussy, *Kraftwerk: Man, Machine and Music* (London, 2001), pp. 64–5.

4   Willi Andresen, 'Computer Liebe'. Interview with Ralf Hütter, *Tip*, 22 (1991), p. 202.

5   Mike Beecher, 'Kraftwerk Revealed'. Interview with Ralf Hütter, *Electro Music Magazine*, 9 (1981), p. 8.

6   Cf. http://www.simsi.net/4680/4734.html.

7   Quoted in Bussy, *Kraftwerk*, p. 69.

8   Ibid., p. 86.

9   Neil Straus, 'Call Them The Beatles of Electronic Dance Music', *The New York Times*, 15 June 1997.

10 Quoted in David Buckley, *Kraftwerk: Publikation* (London, 2012), p. 161.

11 Jäki Eldorado, quoted in Rudi Esch, *Electri_City: The Düsseldorf School of Electronic Music* (London, 2016), p. 156.

12 Ibid., p. 23.

13 Geeta Dayal, 'Kraftwerk on Cycling, 3D, "Spiritual Connection" to Detroit'. Interview with Ralf Hütter, *Rolling Stone* (US), 8 (2015).

14 Quoted in Barr, *Kraftwerk*, p. 120.

15 Cf. *Die Hifi Stereo-Kulisse – 98 Geräusche für den Film- und Tonbandfreund*, Polydor 1973.

16 Buckley, p. 268.

17 Ibid., p. 95.

18 Quoted in Bussy, *Kraftwerk*, p. 28.

19 Ibid., p. 163.

20 Robert Fink, 'The Story of ORCH5, or, the Classical Ghost in the Hip-Hop Machine', in *Popular Music*, 24 (2005), p. 352.

21 Bussy, *Kraftwerk*, p. 94.

22 Barr, *Kraftwerk*, p. 172.

23 Quoted in Urich Adelt, *Krautrock: German Music in the Seventies* (Michigan, 2016), p. 138.

24 Peter Shapiro, *Turn the Beat Around: The Rise and Fall of Disco* (London, 2005), pp. 109–11.

25 Barr, *Kraftwerk*, p. 19.

26 After Cybotron, Atkins would continue as Model 500, scoring a club hit with his first single 'No UFOs' (1985), but he also released music under the moniker Infinity

during the first half of the nineties. Still going strong today, the Model 500 album *Digital Solutions* was one of the best techno releases of 2015.

27 Quoted in Mark Fisher, interview with Mike Banks, *Wire*, 285 (2007).

28 Christoph Schaub, 'Beyond the Hood? Detroit Techno, Underground Resistance, and African-American Metropolitan Identity Politics', *Forum for Inter-American Research*, 2:2 (2009).

29 David Stubbs, *Mars by 1980: The Story of Electronic Music* (London, 2018), p. 249.

30 Mark Dery (ed.), *Flame Wars: The Discourse of Cyberculture* (Durham, NC, 1994), p. 180.

31 After the death of Stinson, Gerald Donald has released music under various aliases and project names. Once he was liberated from the conceptual restraints of the Drexciya project, the considerable Kraftwerk influence on the producer became even clearer. His most well-known moniker is the duo Dopplereffekt, founded in 1995, which features numerous German references in an unmistakeable nod to Kraftwerk. For instance, *Gesamtkunstwerk* was chosen for the title of their 1999 compilation of tracks, which betray such evident proximity to the Kraftwerk sound that they occasionally sound like persiflage of the original.

32 Simon Witter, 'Paranoid Androids?'. Interview with Ralf Hütter, *Mojo*, 9 (2005).

8. Postscript: 1 2 3 4 5 6 7 8

1 Tim Jonze, 'Music is about Intensity . . . the Rest is Just Noise'. Interview with Ralf Hütter, *Guardian*, 15 June 2017.

2 Ed Power, 'Ghost in the Machine'. Interview with Ralf Hütter, *Independent* (Ireland), 12 July 2013.